365 SURFBOARDS

BEN MARCUS

MVP
BOOKS

First published in 2013 by MVP Books, an imprint of MBI Publishing Company, 400 First Avenue North, Suite 400, Minneapolis, MN 55401 USA

MVP Books titles are also available at discounts in bulk quantity for industrial or sales-promotional use.
For details write to Special Sales Manager at Quayside Publishing Group, 400 First Avenue North, Suite 400, Minneapolis, MN 55401 USA.

To find out more about our books, visit us online at www.mvpbooks.com.

Library of Congress Cataloging-in-Publication Data
Marcus, Ben, 1960-
  365 surfboards : the coolest, raddest, most innovative boards from around the world / Ben Marcus.
      pages cm
  Summary: "A history of surfboards offering images and descriptions of the most important, innovative, or interesting surfboards from throughout the world"-- Provided by publisher.
   ISBN 978-0-7603-4529-0 (pbk.)
  1. Surfboards--History. 2. Surfboards--Collectibles. 3. Surfing--History. I. Title. II. Title: Three hundred and sixty- five surfboards.
  GV840.S8M273 2013
  797.3'2--dc23
                            2013028492

On the front cover: Surfboard photos by Juliana Morais. Background photo courtesy of Shutterstock.com.

Editor: Josh Leventhal
Design Manager: James Kegley
Layout by: Erin Fahringer
Design by: Simon Larkin

Printed in China

Preface

From *olo* and *alaia* to carbon fiber and epoxy, by way of koa, redwood, spruce, cedar, pine, balsa, polyurethane foam, and polyester resin. The following pages detail the evolution of the surfboard from ancient *Owyhee* to the high-tech present—board by board, era by era, evolution by revolution. Planks, kookboxes, scarfed noses, Malibu chips, Greenough spoons, Bonzers, Thrusters, Quads, sandwich construction, and all the way back to the modern olo and alaia being made by craftsmen around the world today.

This book came together fast, and to pull it all together required a great deal of begging, borrowing, and bartering for surfboards from shapers, surfers, and collectors. And I had help. A lot of people I knew and a lot of people I didn't know contributed hundreds of photos of surfboards past, present, and future, and thousands of words of information on those boards. I couldn't have done this book without them, and I want to try and thank them all right here.

Thanks to Glenn Sakamoto at liquidsaltmag.com and Zach Weisberg at theinertia.com for helping to get the word out, and also to Michael Paler at the surfboard shapers site Swaylocks.com. Also thanks to everyone who kicked in dough on Kickstarter and Indiegogo.

Lucia Griggi photographed many of the portraits you see in this book, as well as many of the surfboards from collectors like Griff Snyder and John Mazza. During the course of this book, I sent 602 emails to Lucia, and I want to apologize for that, and thank her for her hard work.

Juliana Morais shot beautiful images of Fernando Aguerre's collection for my earlier book, *The Surfboard: Art, Style, Stoke,* and many of those glorious photos are seen again here.

Listed in order of number of emails sent and received, I want to thank Steve Ogles, John Mazza, Griff Snyder, Athena Shlien, Joe McGovern, Greg Lui-Kwan, Fernando Aguerre, Cory Bluemling, Alex Williams, Bird Huffman, Mark Fragale, Gerry Lopez, Barry Haun, Michael Paler, Tom Parrish, Mike Tabeling, George Orbelian, Bev and Connie Morgan, and Bing Copeland.

There is a long, long list of others who helped, and at risk of leaving someone out, as you read the book, you will see names like Sid Abruzzi, Pete Pan, Shaun Tomson, Randy Rarick, Barry Haun, Greg and Laura Noll, Wingnut, Bruce Brown, Dick Metz, Spencer Croul, and Matt Warshaw—those people all deserve thanks.

Elizabeth Pepin shot portraits in Hawaii and California, so thanks to her and also to Nikki Brooks for kicking in a lot of photos she had in her files.

Some people I didn't know—like Joe McGovern on the East Coast and Greg Lui-Kwan in Hawaii—came through with dozens of photos of boards. Jimmy Buffett is to surfboards what Imelda Marcos is to shoes and Jerry Seinfeld is to Porsches. He has a great collection that is on display at the Honolulu Surfing Museum. By way of Mark Fragale at the Honolulu Surfing Museum and Barry Haun at the Surfing Heritage and Cultural Center, Jimmy let us use two dozen of his best boards. Thanks for that.

Alex Williams kept up the British end, and hopefully people in the U.K. will enjoy this book for his efforts. Bev Morgan, whom I now refer to as the Photo Deity, and his daughter Connie were very generous at flowing images I needed—and sometimes couldn't believe existed. I asked, and they delivered.

I could write a book about writing *365 Surfboards* and the stories behind the stories are pretty interesting: Tom Parrish's thoughts on all things surfboard, Felipe Pomar arguing for Peru, Corky Carroll and Bob McTavish and others arguing the Shortboard Revolution. A lot of stories.

There were also some good deeds along the way. It was cool to reunite Tony Moniz with his long-lost Aipa gun, and Bernie Ross with her Downing. Thanks to Bernie for the *kala*.

Five months, hundreds of surfboards, thousands of emails, and tens of thousands of words later, what you have in your hands is a graphic timeline of the surfboard, from olo and alaia to epoxy and carbon fiber—the definitive book on the evolution of the surfboard. It was a lot of work, and I hope it was all worth it. Again I want to thank everyone who helped get 'er done.

Origins in Three Parts

This triptych of surfboards shows the Polynesian pursuit of *he'e nalu* (surfing) from Polynesia's *Owyhee* (Hawaii) to Captain James Cook's Sandwich Islands to the 20th century Hawaiian Islands. The board for *Origins 1* was made by Alan Leftwick of Solana Beach from white pine with koa rail panels. The boards for *Origins 2* (pine) and *Origins 3* (mahogany) were made by Chris Simpson. According to Southern California surfer/artist Wade Koniakowsky, the template for the second two boards was taken from a pre-revival *alaia* board at the Bernice Pauahi Bishop Museum, the Hawaii State Museum of Natural and Cultural History in Honolulu, and given to Simpson by the legendary shaper for Harbour, Mike Marshall.

"When I decided to paint an *alaia*," Koniakowsky said, "I thought since it was an ancient design, the images should delve into the roots of surfing—all the way back to Captain Cook, Duke Kahanamoku, and the famous shot of the guy standing at Waikiki holding an *alaia*. I mixed this with other various Polynesian flora and fauna, graphics and depictions of perfect waves, all of which seemed to work in paying homage to the origins of the sport."

The boards were done in a mix of media, including acrylic paint, gold leaf, and block prints, and then finished with clear, water-based varnish.

Origins 1   Origins 2   Origins 3

Courtesy Wade Koniakowsky

Tahitian Bronze

Tahitians getting their kicks riding waves was first described in 1769 by Sir Joseph Banks, an adventurous English aristocrat who paid his own way on Captain James Cook's first voyage of discovery aboard *The Endeavor*, from 1768 to 1771. Eight years later, William Anderson was the surgeon on board *The Resolution* for Captain Cook's second voyage into the Pacific. Anderson recorded in the ship's log these impressions of watching a surf-rider, words that have long been attributed to Cook, but are no less eloquent: "I could not help concluding that this man felt the most supreme pleasure while he was driven on so fast and so smoothly by the sea."

Wade Koniakowsky's *Tahitian Bronze* was produced in 2009, the year that Dick Brewer was the featured shaper at the Sacred Craft surfboard show. "Brewer sent me a bunch of boards—tow-in, guns, etc.," said Koniakowsky. "That little board was a standard-issue Brewer Thruster, maybe 6 feet, 3 inches. It was painted in acrylic metallic paint, along with variegated gold leaf. Polynesians are a big part of my art, and Tahitian women are some of the most inspired subjects in the realm of figure painting."

Caballito de Totora, 3000 BC

Peruvian Jose "Kane" Ramos reads the drop on a board made of reeds at a bombora peak that forms at the end of the pier in Huanchaco, Peru.

As far back as 3000 BC, Peruvian fishermen have been paddling these watercraft they called *tup* and the Spanish *conquistadores* called *caballito de totora* or "little horses made of reeds." They were made for practical purposes—fishing, trade, transportation—but some argue that the coastal Peruvians were the first surfers. Peruvian Felipe Pomar, a former World Surfing Champion, contends his ancestors rode waves for commerce and for pleasure—racing to shore with fresh fish thousands of years ago.

Also shown is South Bay adventurer and movie mogul Joel T. Smith posing with a quiver of *caballito de totora* on the beach at Huanchaco, Peru. An average *caballito* is 12 feet long by 2 feet wide and weighs 90 pounds.

African Board from Sao Tome

In the 2007 documentary, *The Lost Wave*, surfers Sam George, Joe Curren, and Holly Beck and producer Paul Taublieb traveled to a far corner of deepest Africa—to the island of Sao Tome—to find a group of local kids led by a native wave rider named Chum. These kids were riding waves on pieces of wood that didn't seem to have any connection to the 21st or even the 20th century, and Sam believed he had found an indigenous African sport. He saw a chance to "rewrite surfing's historical timeline." This experience offered a firsthand description of an indigenous surf culture, adding an African surfing story to the traditional Polynesian paradigm.

"An extraordinary discovery," George effuses in the film's narration. "A totally unique, undiscovered surfing culture. Here was a group of adolescent boys who rode waves in front of their tiny, thatched-hut village. These young Africans had seen very few white men, and never another surfer. . . . This was the first [Western] contact with completely indigenous surfers since James Cook landed in Hawaii in 1778."

Here George poses in his Malibu home with an example of an African wave-riding vehicle.

Photo by Lucia Griggi

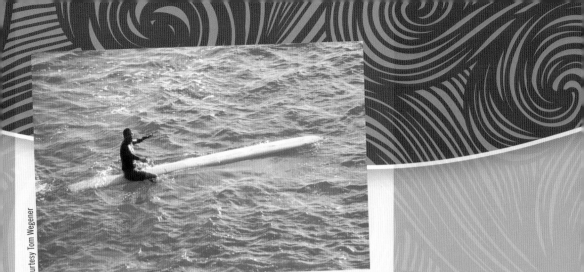

Tom Wegener's Hawaiian Quiver

Tom Wegener's collection of surfboards goes back to the ancient Hawaiian surfboard—or *papa he'e nalu*, and here he poses outside his home with six from his personal quiver. The 19th-century Hawaiian historian John Papa I'i described the three main types of ancient Hawaiian boards: "The *olo* is thick in the middle and grows thinner toward the edges. It is a good board for a wave that swells and rushes shoreward but not for a wave that rises up high and curls over. The *kiko'o* reaches a length of 12 to 18 feet and is good for a surf that breaks roughly. The *alaia* board, which is 9 feet long, is thin and wide in front, tapering toward the back. Because it tends to go downward and cut through a wave, it does not rise up with the wave as it begins to curl over. Skilled surfers use it frequently, but the unskilled are afraid of this board, choosing rather to sit on a canoe or to surf on even smaller boards [*papa li'ili'i*]."

Tom Wegener
first wave on the Olo
Wategos, Autumn 2006
frame grabs by Nathan Oldfield

Courtesy Tom Wegener

In 2009, *Surfing Magazine* named Wegener "Shaper of the Year" for introducing a new generation to what Hawaiians called *lala*, which translates to "the controlled slide in the curl when surfing on a board." The American-born Wegener moved to Noosa, Australia, in 1998, and discovered a local Australian wood called Paulownia, which he used to make traditional Hawaiian boards. Over the next four years, Wegener made more than 300 hollow, wood-finned surfboards.

"In 2004, I was very busy with custom orders for my hollow-wood noseriders," he recalled. "I had lots of orders, and they were all $3,000 boards. For a moment I was on top. So I took the family on a trip to Waikiki to surf the wood boards with the spirits of Tom Blake and the Duke. After reading the book *Tom Blake: The Uncommon Journey of a Pioneer Waterman* and Blake's own book *Surfing 1936*, I hoped to go and template Chief Paki's *olo* and make one for myself."

After visiting the Bishop Museum in Honolulu, Wegener made his *olo* to the exact dimensions of Chief Paki's *olo*, except Wegener's is an even 16 feet long while Paki's was just over 15½ feet. Both are 18½ inches wide and 6½ inches thick. "My *olo* weighs over 150 pounds," Wegener explained. "It takes two people to lift it and three people to put it on its tail. Chief Paki's *olo* is made from koa wood and is solid."

Wegener struggled at first to ride the *olo*, but he finally got some very memorable rides, including the sequence shown here from 2006. "It took a long time to figure out how to surf it. Your feet have to be hanging over the tail of the board when you catch the wave. It is a big challenge to surf, but it is sure worth it!"

Greg Noll's Modern 12' 6" *Olo*

This 12-foot, 6-inch solid koa board was shaped by Greg "Da Bull" Noll as a tribute to the ancient Hawaiians. Only the *ali'i* (royalty) were allowed to surf *olo*—and some say the punishment was death for a commoner riding the board of an *ali'i*. These were very rare and special boards.

This most precious koa wood was hand-picked by Greg during a trip to the Big Island of Hawaii. It's illegal to harvest live koa, so when a tree dies or falls, people like Greg fly to Hawaii to pick planks. This koa plank was aged for two years before Noll shaped the *olo* using specifications from boards stored in the Bernice Pauahi Bishop Museum in Honolulu.

This board is one of many in Fernando Aguerre's collection. Originally from Argentina, Aguerre was one of the founders, along with his brother Santiago, of the surf brand Reef in 1984.

Twenty years later, the Aguerre brothers sold Reef to Vanity Fair Corporation. Fernando now lives in a surfer's dream home: a cozy beach shack on La Jolla's "Street of Dreams." Big Rock and Windansea beaches are visible off to the right, and a whole lot of Pacific Ocean reflects off the white walls of his home, which is filled with surf art and artifacts from around the world. He has a dreamy collection of more than 100 surfboards—from original and re-created *olo* and *alaia* to modern thrusters from the likes of Kelly Slater, Rob Machado, Rochelle Ballard, and Andy Irons.

Photo by Lucia Griggi

Photo by Juliana Morais; Board courtesy Fernando Aguerre

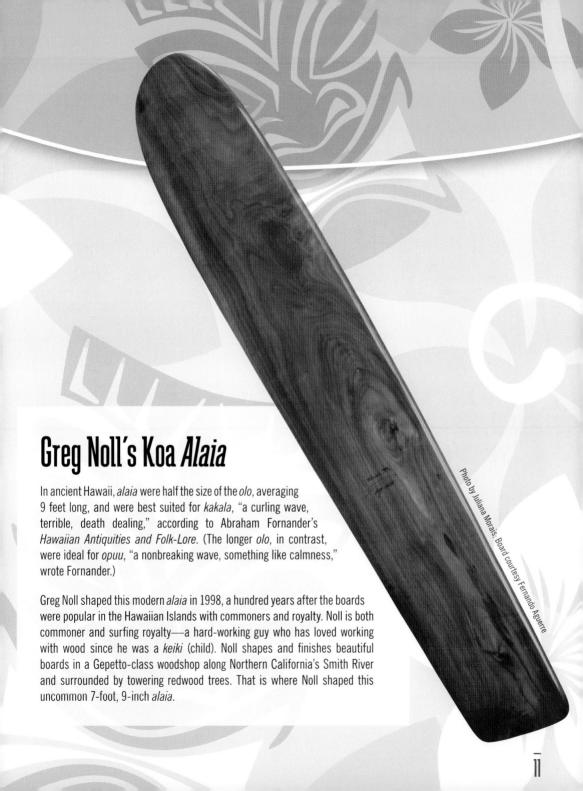

Greg Noll's Koa *Alaia*

In ancient Hawaii, *alaia* were half the size of the *olo*, averaging 9 feet long, and were best suited for *kakala*, "a curling wave, terrible, death dealing," according to Abraham Fornander's *Hawaiian Antiquities and Folk-Lore*. (The longer *olo*, in contrast, were ideal for *opuu*, "a nonbreaking wave, something like calmness," wrote Fornander.)

Greg Noll shaped this modern *alaia* in 1998, a hundred years after the boards were popular in the Hawaiian Islands with commoners and royalty. Noll is both commoner and surfing royalty—a hard-working guy who has loved working with wood since he was a *keiki* (child). Noll shapes and finishes beautiful boards in a Gepetto-class woodshop along Northern California's Smith River and surrounded by towering redwood trees. That is where Noll shaped this uncommon 7-foot, 9-inch *alaia*.

The Prayer

While working as lead designer for the Hawaii Maritime Museum on Oahu, Ron Croci was looking through an English–Hawaiian translation dictionary from the 1800s and found a prayer that Hawaiian *kahuna* used to bring up the surf. "Hawaiians used to beat the water with the *pohuehue* vine and chant this prayer," Croci said. The prayer itself is burned on the deck of this board; a small brass plaque below it provides a translation:

If there is no surf, invoke seaward:
Arise! Arise! You great surfs from Kahiki,
The powerful curling waves!
Arise with the pohuehue,
Well up long-raging surf.

Board courtesy Ron Croci

Board courtesy Ron Croci

Tahitian Fantasy

Ron Croci's *Tahitian Fantasy* is a 9-foot balsa board shaped by Robert August and depicting a modern image of a traveling surfer in Tahiti. "In the background," Croci explained, "one can see the beautiful powerboat that transports the surfers to the reef break. The transparency of the dye application as well as the non-painted open sections allows the balsa wood to show through."

Modern *Alaia*

John Mazza is a Malibu resident and surfboard collector who kindly submitted some beautiful specimens for this book, beginning with this rogue's gallery of five replica *alaia*. The craftsmanship of these boards suggests a deep understanding of wave mechanics among early Hawaiians. Made of Chinese cedar, these replicas were commissioned by Mazza and made by surfer and woodworker John Porter and shaper Tommy Nellis. They were based on original Hawaiian boards held in Honolulu's Bishop Museum. The boards measure (left to right): 4 feet, 7 inches long by 12 inches wide; 6 feet, 6 inches long by 14 inches wide; 7 feet, 4 inches long by 17 inches wide; 8 feet by 18 inches wide; 10 feet, 7 inches long by 18 inches wide.

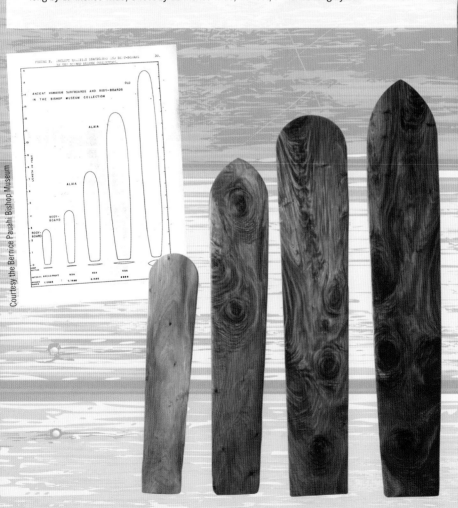

Ulu Paipo

This *paipo* (bellyboard) is the oldest board in the collection of Malibu collector John Mazza, who bought it at Randy Rarick's Hawaiian Islands Vintage Surf Auction in 2005. The catalog described is as a 4-foot, 2-inch *ulu* (breadfruit) board from the late 1800s: "This is a super unique find! An all-original, untouched *ulu* wood bellyboard that was discovered in Waimanalo. It was used in the shore break at Waimanalo and what is now Bellows Field and is scooped up in the nose on the bottom and hollowed out on the deck. The pre-cursor to the modern boogie board? A great piece of Hawaiian surf craft." Rarick got the board from the yard of an old Hawaiian family, and Mazza paid top dollar for it. "This is the real deal," Mazza said.

1900 Hawaiian 8' 10"
Redwood Plank

This 8-foot, 10-inch-long Hawaiian redwood plank was found under an old house near Black Point on the south shore of Oahu. The deck is flat with rounded rails. The board is indicative of a kind of board detailed in *Surfing: A History of the Ancient Hawaiian Sport* by Ben Finney and James Houston, first published in 1966 and revised in 1996. According to Finney and Houston, boards around the turn of the century were made by "Caucasians who fostered the revival at Waikiki." The authors describe boards, similar to the first *alaia* copy, that appeared on Waikiki beaches in 1910: "They were some seven feet long and resembled the short *alaia*. They were two-to-three inches thick, flat on top, with a slightly convex bottom and rounded edges."

The easy access to imported redwood, pine, and other imports replaced koa, *wiliwili*, and other native woods. Where the Hawaiians used burnt *kukui*-nut juice to finish and seal surfboards, this new breed of mainland-inspired board was finished with marine varnish. This plank might have been painted with the bull's head ornament added later.

Photo by Juliana Morais; Board courtesy Fernando Aguerre

7′ 6″ Waikiki Plank

As the population of Hawaii shrank dramatically between the time of Captain James Cook's first visit in the 1770s and the early 20th century, the sport of surfing was declining with it. Then a renaissance of surfing began in Waikiki in the early 20th century, and the Waikiki plank surfboard became the board of choice. According to Planksurfboards.com, "This new board was designed and developed using what oral traditions were left and the new materials available. The indigenous woods of Hawaii were being phased out for the more abundant and cheaper lumber from mainland USA. Redwood became the lumber of choice, but cedar and pine were used as well." The first Waikiki planks were between 6 and 8 feet in length. After about 1910, they increased in size, to 10 to 12 feet, with outlines similar to the *alaia*.

This classic 7-foot, 6-inch Waikiki plank was unearthed during the cleaning of a house on the North Shore of Oahu. It was authenticated as dating from 1895 to 1900 by the Bishop Museum and was adopted into Fernando Aguerre's collection in 2001.

Photos by Juliana Morais; Board courtesy Fernando Aguerre

Greg Noll's 10' 6" Redwood Plank

In 1996, Greg Noll shaped this facsimile of Duke Kahanamoku's 10-foot, 6-inch redwood plank, which was on display at the Bishop Museum for many years. Noll was allowed access to the original board and took exact measurements; then, he re-created the board from a prime redwood slab.

Born in Honolulu in 1890, Duke Paoa Kahinu Mokoe Hulikohola Kahanamoku grew up surfing and swimming along the beaches of Waikiki. By 1908, he and his Hawaiian friends formed the Hui Nalu, a surfing, swimming, paddling, and canoeing club to compete against the *haole*-owned Outrigger Canoe Club. At the first Hawaiian Amateur Athletic Union swimming and diving championship, held in 1911, Duke broke the world record for the 100-yard freestyle by 4.5 seconds. He then went to Philadelphia and easily qualified for the U.S. Olympic team that traveled to Sweden for the 1912 summer games in Stockholm. He set a world record and won gold in the 100-meter freestyle and silver in the 200-meter relay. Duke quickly became world famous, and he made the Hawaiian Islands and the sport of surf riding famous in his wake.

Betty Carstairs 11' 6" Plank

This 11-foot, 6-inch solid redwood plank was one of two gifts to Marion Betty Carstairs from a "Hawaiian King," most likely Hawaiian Prince Jonah Kuhio, in about 1914. Carstairs was a surfing heiress and romantic adventuress. According to Malibu surfboard collector Griff Snyder, Carstairs traveled in "high society" and had affairs with several actresses and notable women of the day, including Marlene Dietrich and Tallulah Bankhead. Her custom planks might have been two of the first surfboards to make it to the Atlantic. The Hawaiian Royal crest is hand-painted on the deck, but the meaning of the black background to the crest and the black band is unknown—possibly a protest to the overthrow of the Hawaiian monarchy.

This board is arguably one of the finest solid wood plank surfboards in a private collection. Carstairs owned two of these boards, but this board is longer than its sibling, now held at the Surfing Heritage and Cultural Center, which is considered one of the most valuable boards in its extensive collection.

1910 Waikiki 9′ 10″ Plank

This 9-foot, 10-inch classic redwood Waikiki plank dates back to 1910. It came to Fernando Aguerre by way of Greg Noll by way of legendary surfer Buffalo Keaulana. As the story goes, Noll was drinking beer at Buffalo's house in Nanakuli. Buffalo's sons Brian and Rusty were playing on the board, standing on it and making surfing poses. Noll offered to trade a case of beer for the board, but Buffalo showed the aloha: "Take 'em, brah." Some Waikiki beach boys dated the board back to 1910 and said it was once part of the fence at Queen's Surf restaurant on the beach at Waikiki.

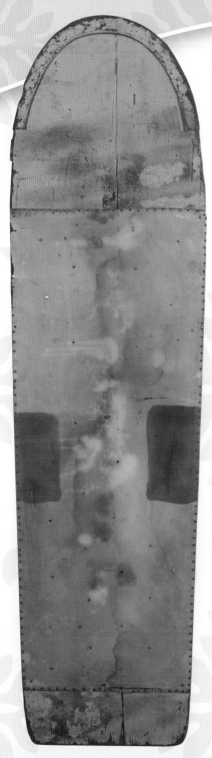

Two Planks circa 1910

These two planks date from about 1910 and are housed in the collection of Fernando Aguerre. The first board (left) was purchased by a U.S. Navy admiral posted in Pearl Harbor. This incredibly rare and unusual board has a metallic nose guard and a canvas piece on the top to prevent sliding over the board or to protect the rider from wood splinters while riding—or both. The second plank is short at 6 feet and very wide. It was part of an East Coast collection.

Photos by Lucia Griggi; Boards courtesy Fernando Aguerre

1910 8' 1" Redwood Plank

Around the turn of the 20th century, materials and design for Hawaiian surfboards began to change as local craftsmen used redwood, pine, and other non-Hawaiian materials to make the boards, and the design evolved from *alaia* to planks. What didn't change was the Hawaiian custom of not adorning surfboards. Hawaiians love to tinker and paint and carve and decorate, but that custom did not extend to surfboards. Some scholars believe that cultural trait goes back to Hawaiian canoes, which were unique in Polynesia for not being decorated or painted much at all. Scholars believe Hawaiians placed function over form in canoes and felt that decoration could weaken a craft, a vessel of life-and-death importance to the Hawaiians. Hawaiian canoes weren't overly adorned, and so surfboards were Plain Jane as well. This redwood plank has a small mark near the tail, but the rest of the board is all redwood grain.

1913 Renny Yater's 15' 5" *Olo* Replica

This 15-foot, 5-inch-long by 19½-inch-wide redwood *olo* is the largest surfboard built by renowned surfboard shaper Reynolds Yater. Yater carved out the board in 1997 using a plan from the catalog of the collection in Honolulu's Bishop Museum dated 1913. It is a reinterpretation of the traditional *olo*, but neither as long nor as thick. Yater shaped this version at the request of James O'Mahoney, a surfboard collector and founder of the Santa Barbara Surf Museum in California. It has never been ridden.

Traditional *olo* boards were made from a variety of native woods, including *ulu* (breadfruit), *wiliwili* (Hawaiian balsa), and strong, hard koa. This board is made of west coast redwood. But even there is a connection to the ancient Hawaiian tradition: redwood logs would occasionally wash up on Hawaiian shores after drifting for years in the Pacific. Such logs were highly valued as a material for surfboards, including *olo*, and were revered as *ho-okupu ke kai*—divine gifts from the sea.

1915 Duke Kahanamoku's Australian Plank

If the surfing world has a holy relic, Duke Kahanamoku's 1915 surfboard could be it. For the celebration of Surfing Australia's 50th anniversary, Duke's board was taken out of its glass case at Sydney's Freshwater Surf Life Saving Club, and it attracted the likes of Kelly Slater, Tom Carroll, Mark Richards, Layne Beachley, and Australian Deputy Prime Minister Wayne Swan.

In 1915, Duke accepted an invitation from the New South Wales Swimming Association to visit Australia. Duke landed in Sydney after a two-week passage on a steamship from Hawaii, saw surf, and most likely regretted leaving his plank back home. He had a week to kill with no official duties, so at Sydney timber supplier George Hudson's, Duke found a good piece of imported sugar pine that was 9 feet long, 2 feet wide, and 3 inches thick. The lumberyard cut out a board to Duke's template, and he finished an 8-foot by 23-inch by 3-inch plank that weighed 78 pounds.

The board stayed in Australia and was mastered by Claude West, who dominated surf club competitions from 1915 to 1922 and became Australia's first board-riding champion. In 1953 West donated the board to the Freshwater Surf Life Saving Club, and at some point, the metal letters and pinlines were added to commemorate the board. West restored the board in 1976 after it fell off a truck and split in two.

at "Boomerang" Freshwater. Janu

1918 Redwood Hawaiian 4' 7" Plank

In 1885, three Hawaiian princes attending a military school in San Mateo, California, made their way to Santa Cruz and fashioned traditional Hawaiian surfboards from local redwood. Jonah Kuhio and his brothers made history as the first reported "surf swimmers" on the West Coast, but they probably weren't the first Hawaiians to work with redwood. By the turn of the 20th century, Hawaiians had discovered that redwood was much easier to work with than native Hawaiian hardwoods, and more and more Hawaiian surfboards were made from the wood from the land beyond the eastern horizon. This 4-foot, 7-inch traditional Hawaiian plank is made from nontraditional redwood.

Photo by Juliana Morais; Board courtesy Fernando Aguerre

Long Beach Bellyboard

This 3-foot-long wooden bellyboard from the 1920s was available for rent on Long Beach, California, during a time before many of the breakwaters were built and waves broke in places that are now developed with piers, amusement parks, and condo complexes.

Photo by Juliana Morais; Board courtesy Fernando Aguerre

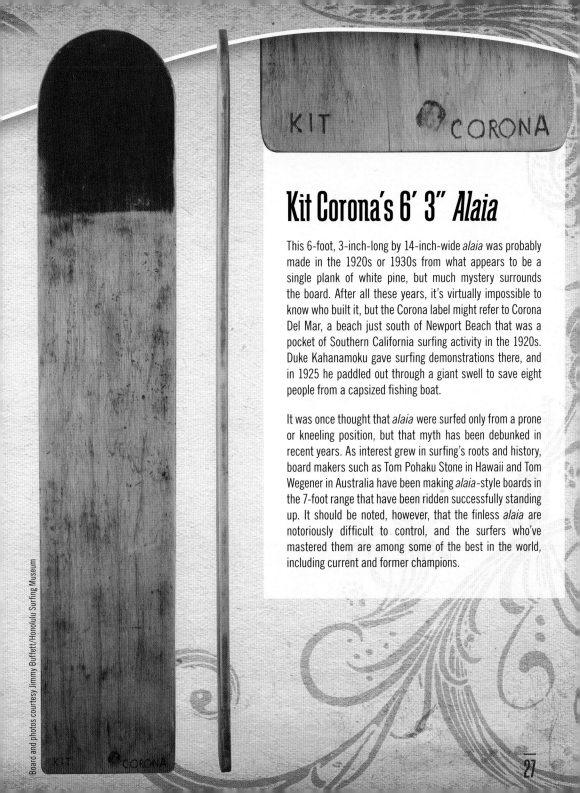

KIT   CORONA

Kit Corona's 6' 3" *Alaia*

This 6-foot, 3-inch-long by 14-inch-wide *alaia* was probably made in the 1920s or 1930s from what appears to be a single plank of white pine, but much mystery surrounds the board. After all these years, it's virtually impossible to know who built it, but the Corona label might refer to Corona Del Mar, a beach just south of Newport Beach that was a pocket of Southern California surfing activity in the 1920s. Duke Kahanamoku gave surfing demonstrations there, and in 1925 he paddled out through a giant swell to save eight people from a capsized fishing boat.

It was once thought that *alaia* were surfed only from a prone or kneeling position, but that myth has been debunked in recent years. As interest grew in surfing's roots and history, board makers such as Tom Pohaku Stone in Hawaii and Tom Wegener in Australia have been making *alaia*-style boards in the 7-foot range that have been ridden successfully standing up. It should be noted, however, that the finless *alaia* are notoriously difficult to control, and the surfers who've mastered them are among some of the best in the world, including current and former champions.

OCC 11′ 6″ Redwood Plank

The logo on this 11-foot, 6-inch solid redwood plank is for the Outrigger Canoe Club, which was established in 1908 on a beachfront lot where the Royal Hawaiian Hotel now stands. The purpose of the club was to revitalize the dying Hawaiian arts of canoe paddling and surfing and make a place where "men and boys could ride upright on the crest of waves." The board was built in the 1920s, serving the club into the 1940s. After its useful years, the board was used as a decorative totem at the entrance before being removed when the club was relocated closer to Diamond Head. A collector named Joe Alphabet owned the board for many years, and then it passed to Fernando Aguerre.

1925 10′ Cedar Plank

Raw cedar planks made it to the Hawaiian Islands around 1925, and the local craftsmen saw that cedar was good for making surfboards. This 10-foot solid cedar plank was hand-shaped on the beach in Waikiki. This was close to the time Tom Blake came to Hawaii and revolutionized the surfboard by making hollow *olo*-inspired modern surfboards. Wood planks like this soon became passé, and the board was left unwanted under a tree in the Manoa Valley for 60 years.

1920s California Planked Plank

This board was labeled as a "plank" when sent to John Mazza for captioning help, but he objected to the label. "I'm not sure if it can be called a plank, since it is made of 1- to 1½-inch strips that are held together with the three horizontal bars," Mazza explained. "The term 'plank' refers to a piece of wood that is flat with no rocker. A plank of wood is solid, flat, and straight. This board has the shape of a 'plank' but is not one piece of wood. . . . It is waxed, not varnished, and has flexibility that a plank would not have. I am sure it is a homemade board by someone who knew how to work with wood." Mazza suspects that it is from the Santa Monica region of California, dating from the mid to late 1920s. "It is definitely unique," he added.

Photo by Lucia Griggi; Board courtesy John Mazza

Southern California Cedar Plank

In the early 1900s, the *Los Angeles Times* ran a photo of a beach crowd near one of the Santa Monica piers, which clearly shows a guy walking up the beach with a Hawaiian plank surfboard. Many people traveled back and forth from California to Hawaii for business and pleasure during the late 19th and early 20th centuries, so it's not surprising that there are plank surfboards scattered around Southern California. This board was found in the garage of a house that was being torn down in Santa Monica. "It is probably cedar," said John Mazza. "It could be pine, since it is light, but there are no known holes. From the design of the tail I would put it around 1920."

1920s Plank

The horizontal bar across the top of this plank board looks similar to the one on a board that George Freeth is holding in a photo taken around 1907. But it's probably not that board, according to John Mazza, who estimates that this board dates from about 1925. "The shape is definitely about that time," Mazza said. "The board is not a *paipo*/bellyboard. I am pretty sure it was intended as a short *alaia*. Whoever owned it ruffed up the deck near the tail to provide traction to stand. . . . In person, it looks really old and has a great patina that is not weather related but rather just old, old wood." Mazza pointed out that the board has two holes hand-drilled in it for a rod handle, but they appear to be a later addition. "My best guess is that it is mid to late 1920s, although it could be older."

Half Hawaiian and half Irish, Freeth was "discovered" by Jack London while surfing Waikiki in 1907. Freeth left Hawaii soon after and traveled to Southern California. Freeth put on surfing exhibitions at Redondo Beach and Venice as the "Man Who Can Walk on Water." Ocean drownings were epidemic during the early 1900s, and as a surfer, swimmer, diver, lifeguard, and trainer, Freeth passed his ocean knowledge and safety and rescue skills to the public and to a young generation of West Coast watermen, laying down a foundation of ocean safety that has saved countless lives over the century.

Courtesy the Bernice Pauahi Bishop Museum

Photo by Lucia Griggi; Board courtesy John Mazza

Shark-Inlaid
10′ Redwood Plank

Dr. Richard Arnest was the original owner of this 10-foot Waikiki redwood plank from the 1920s, and he surfed Waikiki on it through the 1930s. In the 1950s, his son cut the shark inlay to the deck, preparing it to be a bar top. But that never happened, and the board retains its original form and function.

Two Short 1930s Planks

The expression "thick as two short planks" can refer to someone's intelligence or lack thereof. But the intelligence on these two planks came from collector John Mazza: "I bought these as a pair from a guy in Arizona who said that his father was in the navy at Pearl Harbor. [The board] with the lady on it was his sister's and the other was his, and he said his father bought them as 'kids' boards' in the mid-1930s." The boards are totally flat planks, with no rocker or steam nose.

Photo by Lucia Griggi; Boards courtesy John Mazza

Redwood and Spruce 10' 8" Plank

Just as redwood usurped koa and *wiliwili* as the surfboard material of choice in the early 20th century, by the 1930s, surfboard makers were experimenting with other woods. This 10-foot, 8-inch plank is laminated with redwood and spruce. Redwood weighs between 28.08 and 31.82 pounds per cubic foot. Spruce is 28 pounds per cubic foot. Red cedar is about 23 pounds per cubic foot. Because 40 percent of balsa is air trapped in cells, it ranges from 6 to 19 pounds per cubic foot.

Board and photo courtesy the John Mazza Historical Surfboard Collection, Pepperdine University Special Collections and University Archives

1933
11′ 6″ Redwood Bar Top

This 11-foot, 6-inch redwood laminated plank is an early example of a lighter weight plank that was made using chambered, laminated construction. Late in its life, the board was used as a bar top (you can see screw holes from the screwballs who turned this beauty into furniture). It was restored to its proper use and dignity.

Midcentury *Paipo*

These two bellyboards are in the collection of John Mazza, who described the one on the left as a "ragged *paipo*." "I bought this from a *hapa-haole* guy on the South Shore," Mazza explained. "He said it had been around his house since he was a kid. . . . He thought the board belonged to his grandfather. I believe it was always a *paipo*, and from the construction [one-piece redwood, no glue, and thin], I think it is early 1930s. Whoever made it got it really flat, but it does not appear to have been machine planed."

The board on the right is homemade with Marine plywood about ¾ inches thick. It likely dates from the 1930s or 1940s.

Ironing Board Surfboard

If it looks like an ironing board and floats like an ironing board, then maybe that's what it is. This one bears a logo for the Long Beach Surf Club. According to John Mazza, "The LBSC board is a 1920s or '30s ironing board. It's as simple as that. . . . I did find references in some 1930s material about kids using ironing boards to surf. I have an LA Ladder ironing board that I bought just to have LA Ladder material. This ironing board is longer but basically the same shape, and looks to be made in the late '30s."

George O'Brien's 9′ 1″ Waikiki Special

This 9-foot, 1-inch-long by 22-inch-wide varnished balsa and redwood board was reportedly owned by or loaned to Hollywood actor George O'Brien. The handsome silent-film star visited Waikiki in 1931 and stayed at the Royal Hawaiian Hotel with the great Hollywood director John Ford. While in Waikiki, according to a newspaper report, O'Brien learned "the genuine art of Hawaiian surfing" under instruction from "none other than Duke Kahanamoku, a warm personal friend, while at Hollywood." The newspaper did not say how O'Brien fared in the waves, but it noted: "What a booster he is going to be for the sport!"

This board is inscribed "Moloa" in the Hawaiian tradition of giving boards a spirit name. The meaning connotes laid-back, happy times or even "lazy"—a perfect motto for the beach-boy lifestyle. The board is similar to those produced by Pacific Systems Homes in the early 1930s, but it does not bear that company's mark. So, whether it was made in Hawaii or on the mainland remains a mystery. The shallow wooden fin is almost certainly a later addition.

Board and photos courtesy Jimmy Buffett/Honolulu Surfing Museum

Plank and Aquaplane

The board on the right is not technically a surfboard; it is an ancestor of the water ski or the wake board known as an "aquaplane." In the strict dictionary definition, an aquaplane is a "board pulled over the water by a motorboat and ridden by a person standing up." According to *The Adirondack Almanac*, "Aquaplaning is sometimes cited as beginning around 1920, but it was a common component of boat shows in the United States a decade earlier. In 1909 and 1910, participants attempted to ride a toboggan or an ironing-board-shaped plank, usually about five feet long and two feet wide, towed behind a boat. The boards often resembled the average house door."

The board on the right is an aquaplane, while the board on the left, according to John Mazza, is a plank made of the same plywood as the aquaplane. "The thicker layers of ply indicate it's pre-1950s."

Tom Blake's Quiver

Ten years after Wisconsin native Tom Blake shook the hand of returning Olympian Duke Kahanamoku in Detroit in 1920, Blake stood in Waikiki with a quiver of modern *olo* that would change the surfboard forever. The shortest is an 11-foot redwood "riding board" that was 23 inches wide and 3½ inches thick. Next to that is a 12-footer made of red cedar that Blake used both for surf riding and paddling. Third from the left is one of the hollow *olo* Blake made from boards he had seen in the Bishop Museum in 1926. This board was 14 feet, 6 inches long and 20 inches wide and weighed 120 pounds. The fourth board was *Okohola*, the riding version of his hollow, *olo*-inspired shapes originally made for paddle racing. The last two boards are identical, hollow 16-footers; the one with the Outrigger Canoe Club logo on the deck (second from the right) is a lighter version used for racing, while the sixth board is heavier and was used for training. These boards all evolved from Blake poking around in the Bishop Museum around 1926 and modernizing the long, *olo* boards that had once been the domain of Hawaiian royalty.

Courtesy © Croul Publications

Abner Paki's *Olo*

Today, Tom Blake has many historians/worshippers/devotees, and Sam George is one of them. When shown this undated photo from the Bishop Museum, Sam confirmed that it shows Blake with the Abner Paki *olo* that ignited his fascination with surfboard history and design and inspired his hollow, cigar-board evolution (shown in the 1931 patent application illustration). According to George, the bearded man seen with Blake is Dr. William Brigham, the museum's first director.

George calls this *olo* the "most extraordinary board to survive into the 20th century," noting that it must have had some significance to Brigham, as well, enough for him to pose with it for this formal shot. "My best bet is sometime in the teens," said George on the question of the date of the photo. "Blake shaped his replica in 1929 or '30, and by this time the board had already been relegated to the dusty stacks. I wonder what happened to it? It would have to be the most collectable surfboard on earth."

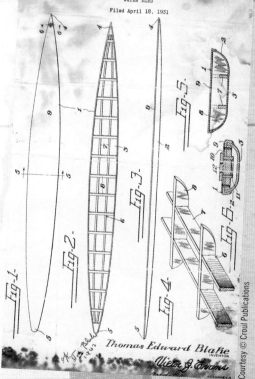

Duke's 16' *Olo*

The Bishop Museum's description of this image is terse: "Duke Kahanamoku standing with his long surfboard in front of the Moana Hotel, Waikiki Beach, Honolulu, Hawaii. Ca. 1930."

If this is 1930, then Duke is 40 years old, fit, and famous as the owner of three gold and two silver medals over three Olympics (1912, 1920, 1924). Duke was 6-foot-1, which would qualify the board he is posing with as an *olo*, and it most likely is the board he made for himself in 1930 based on Tom Blake's innovations. His Blake-inspired design was a 16-footer made of koa wood and weighing 114 pounds. It was designed after the ancient Hawaiian *olo* board, as Blake's had been. Blake praised his friend's handiwork. "He is an excellent craftsman and shapes the lines and balance of his boards with the eye," Blake said. "He detects its irregularities by touch of the hand."

Griff Snyder believes that this might be the 16-foot board that was on display at Duke's Waikiki restaurant for many years.

10′ 11″ Redwood Plank

This 10-foot, 11-inch plank surfboard, currently part of the John Mazza Historical Surfboard Collection at Pepperdine University, is an example of a California-made board from the 1930s. According to the description from Pepperdine, the maker "took advantage of new waterproof glues and balsa wood interlay to lighten the otherwise heavy redwood blank (surfboard core)." The board predates the advent of skegs or fins, but a small skeg was added at a later time. It also looks like someone shaped the nose down a bit, as it's pointier than the typically rounded noses of the time.

Board and photo courtesy John Mazza/Pepperdine University

9′ 6″ Bolted Plank

This 9-foot, 6-inch redwood and pine plank is a fine example of how surfboard makers began to mix hardwoods in the 1930s. The board has bolts along its width to keep the planks from coming apart. The bolts were covered with wooden plugs.

Photo by Juliana Morais. Board courtesy Fernando Aguerre

UK Bellyboards

Bellyboards were popular in the United Kingdom after World War II, according to Tony Cope of the Vintage Surfboard Collector UK blog, as seaside holidays became increasingly popular getaways among the Brits. Woolacombe, on the Devon coast, was one such destination, and a local entrepreneur named Bert Yeo was there waiting for them. Yeo ran a coach tour business, and when the drivers weren't transporting holiday surf and sun seekers, they were cranking out these bellyboards. The boards are 4 feet tall, with an 11-inch tail and a 13-inch nose, and they could get eight of them out of a 4-by-8-foot sheet of marine plywood. Nothing fancy about the design, but they sold like pie and mash.

Bert's nephew Malcolm added that they sold masses of boards to the wholesaler Vince's in Ilfracombe, who sold them on to clients all over England. "Any sandy beach was a potential site for selling or renting out boards," Bert said, "because they could be wedged upright in the sand and used as cricket stumps or windbreaks when the sea was flat. I remember a couple of the names he used on these—Skimmer and Unicorn. If you wanted to hire one it was 10 bob [50 pence] deposit, plus a shilling [5 pence] a day. If one didn't get returned, the deposit pretty well covered the full manufacturing cost!"

Courtesy Alex Williams

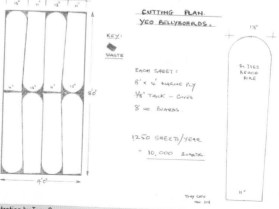

CUTTING PLAN.
YEO BELLYBOARDS.

KEY:

WASTE

EACH SHEET =
8' x 4' MARINE PLY
3/8" THICK – GIVES
8 NO. BOARDS.

1250 SHEETS/YEAR
= 10,000 BOARDS

ST. IVES
BEACH
HIRE

Illustration by Tony Cope

Japanese *Itago* Bellyboards

Domo arigato to Nobuhito "Nobby" Ohkawa, who directed attention to the nobbywoodsurfboards.com website to get the scoop on *itago*. That's the Japanese word for the wooden floor boards that local kids would take from fishing boats as far back as the 1700s and ride waves on them. Hence the name *itago-nori,* which means "floor-board riding."

According to Nobby, the earliest mention of *itago* dates to a haiku poet from Sakata who visited Yunohama Beach in 1821 and saw children shooting the curl on *itago*. "It was not as popular as in Hawaii, where everyone, including kings and queens, enjoyed surfing," Nobby wrote. "That's because in Japan the sea was the place fisherman worked. It was not considered a place for recreation or amusement." Late in the 1800s, bathing beaches were opened for medical purposes only, but soon after, public beaches came to be used for pleasure and leisure activities. "From this period," Nobby concludes, "the *itago* wave riding tool began to be widely made."

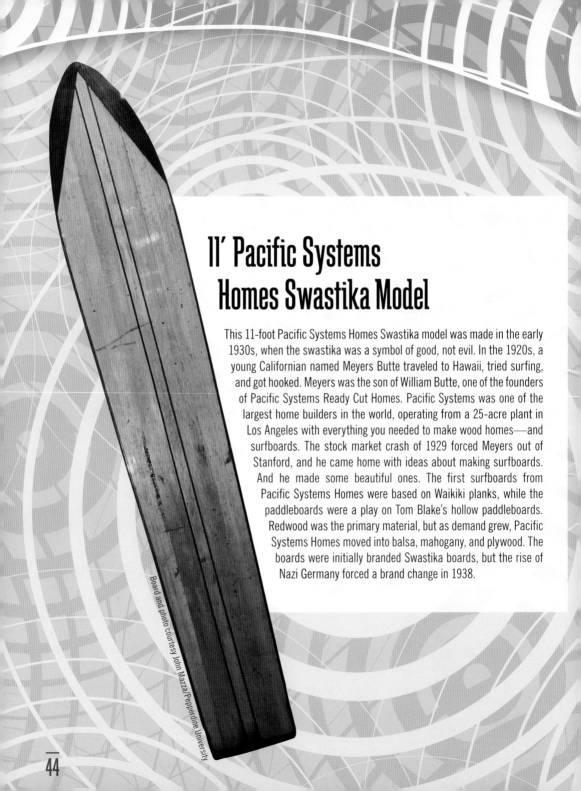

11' Pacific Systems Homes Swastika Model

This 11-foot Pacific Systems Homes Swastika model was made in the early 1930s, when the swastika was a symbol of good, not evil. In the 1920s, a young Californian named Meyers Butte traveled to Hawaii, tried surfing, and got hooked. Meyers was the son of William Butte, one of the founders of Pacific Systems Ready Cut Homes. Pacific Systems was one of the largest home builders in the world, operating from a 25-acre plant in Los Angeles with everything you needed to make wood homes—and surfboards. The stock market crash of 1929 forced Meyers out of Stanford, and he came home with ideas about making surfboards. And he made some beautiful ones. The first surfboards from Pacific Systems Homes were based on Waikiki planks, while the paddleboards were a play on Tom Blake's hollow paddleboards. Redwood was the primary material, but as demand grew, Pacific Systems Homes moved into balsa, mahogany, and plywood. The boards were initially branded Swastika boards, but the rise of Nazi Germany forced a brand change in 1938.

10′ 1″ Replica Swastika Model

Greg Noll shaped this modern replica of a 10-foot, 1-inch Pacific Systems Homes balsa and redwood plank. Noll's modern balsa and redwood board is as well-crafted and beautiful as the originals that came out of Los Angeles in the 1930s. At the time, the boards coming from Pacific Systems Ready Cut Homes were branded with a symbol the Germans called the *hakenkreuz*, or "hooked cross." The symbol is found in cultures, continents, and eras from ancient Greece to India, and it usually is a symbol of good and productivity. The word *swastika* is Sanskrit and translates to "welfare-bringing thing" and that was how the Butte family intended it, as a symbol with "connotations of health and good fortune," according to Wilson, son of Meyers Butte. "My father abandoned it to avoid any controversy soon after Hitler began using it. The Waikiki boards came out around 1938."

11' 4" Early Pete Peterson Balsa Board

This 11-foot, 4-inch by 23½-inch three-wood plank is a very early balsa wood board. It is a one-of-a-kind creation handcrafted by legendary California lifeguard/surfer/shaper/stuntman Preston "Pete" Peterson (1913–1983). Peterson was inspired to use balsa after he first saw the lightweight tropical wood used as a surfboard material while he was visiting Hawaii in 1932. The unique board features a redwood stringer and nose block and a mahogany veneer deck to protect the fragile balsa core.

Peterson was the principal shaper of wooden boards for Pacific Systems Homes, and he may have made this board in their factory. This was Peterson's personal surfboard before it was purchased in 1933 by Dave "Zuke" Simmons. The nickname was painted onto the board by Simmons's brother as a surprise.

Originally, the board was waterproofed by multiple layers of varnish, but sometime in the early 1950s it was coated with a relatively new and much more durable material—fiberglass—by Pacific Glass, among the very first in the trade, and it bears a stamp with the company's logo.

Board and photos courtesy Jimmy Buffett/Honolulu Surfing Museum

10' 9" Refurbished Swastika

This 10-foot, 9-inch Pacific Systems Homes board is made of redwood and balsa with a pine nose block. The original shapers were Pete Peterson and Whitey Harrison. The boards cost $40 in the early 1930s, which was a lot of money during the Depression. (It's equivalent to about $700 in 2013 currency.) As the Nazi Party rose in Germany, surfers fired up their wood burning kits and removed or re-branded that hated swastika symbol. Very few authentic Swastika boards survived World War II; now, 70 years later, a few surfers have fired up their wood burning tools to replace those swastikas.

Jim O'Mahoney restored this board in 1994. He got it from Al Merrick, who had it in his attic in Santa Barbara since the early 1970s. "The board was the McDonalds for many generations of termites," said Mahoney. "A lot of the wood was replaced, and the swastika was re-cut in the new tail wood. . . . I think this is the ultimate Swastika board, especially with the knee slats." Among the shapers and sanders who helped to complete the restoration project were Matt Moore, Alan Gibbons, Chris Kirkegaard, and Tom Long, with historic input from Craig Stecyk and Griff Snyder. The board's tag, *Pua*, refers to the Hawaiian word for flower, but it also can mean "pointy arrow" and "pretty little bundle."

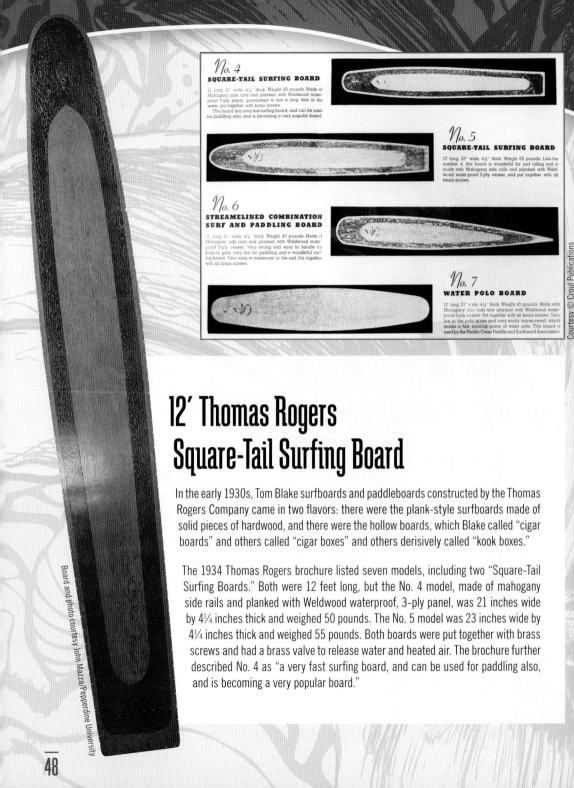

No. 4
SQUARE-TAIL SURFING BOARD

12' long, 21" wide, 4¼" thick. Weight 50 pounds. Made of Mahogany side rails and planked with Weldwood waterproof 3-ply panel, guaranteed to last a long time in the water, put together with brass screws.
This board is a very fast surfing board, and can be used for paddling also, and is becoming a very popular board.

No. 5
SQUARE-TAIL SURFING BOARD

12' long, 23" wide, 4¼" thick. Weight 55 pounds. Like the number 4, this board is wonderful for surf riding and is made with Mahogany side rails and planked with Weldwood water-proof 3-ply veneer, and put together with all brass screws.

No. 6
STREAMLINED COMBINATION SURF AND PADDLING BOARD

12' long, 21" wide, 4¼" thick. Weight 45 pounds. Made of Mahogany side rails and planked with Weldwood waterproof 3-ply veneer. Very strong and easy to handle by boys or girls, very fast for paddling and a wonderful surfing board. Very easy to maneuver in the surf. Put together with all brass screws.

No. 7
WATER POLO BOARD

12' long, 21" wide, 4¼" thick. Weight 45 pounds. Made with Mahogany side rails and planked with Weldwood waterproof 3-ply veneer. Put together with all brass screws. Very fast in the polo game and very easily maneuvered, which makes a fast, exciting game of water polo. This board is used by the Pacific Coast Paddle and Surfboard Association.

12' Thomas Rogers Square-Tail Surfing Board

In the early 1930s, Tom Blake surfboards and paddleboards constructed by the Thomas Rogers Company came in two flavors: there were the plank-style surfboards made of solid pieces of hardwood, and there were the hollow boards, which Blake called "cigar boards" and others called "cigar boxes" and others derisively called "kook boxes."

The 1934 Thomas Rogers brochure listed seven models, including two "Square-Tail Surfing Boards." Both were 12 feet long, but the No. 4 model, made of mahogany side rails and planked with Weldwood waterproof, 3-ply panel, was 21 inches wide by 4¼ inches thick and weighed 50 pounds. The No. 5 model was 23 inches wide by 4¼ inches thick and weighed 55 pounds. Both boards were put together with brass screws and had a brass valve to release water and heated air. The brochure further described No. 4 as "a very fast surfing board, and can be used for paddling also, and is becoming a very popular board."

4' 9" Steamed Nose Redwood

John Mazza bought this 4-foot, 9-inch redwood and pine "steam nose" from Randy Rarick's surf auction in 2009. The auction catalog described it as follows: "This original, multiple-lay-up redwood and pine small plank has an innovative 'steamed nose.' The plank was glued up flat, then the curved nose was created by applying high-temperature steam to create a curve—or kick—in the nose. The rocker that was then created helped to keep the board from 'pearling' or digging in. Has the cut away tail shape, which indicated it was used for riding lying down. A great example of an all-original, period piece small board."

1930s Maine Plank

John Mazza has collected surfboards in the darnedest places. He got this spruce and redwood Pacific Systems Homes—type board in Maine. According to Mazza, a tourist brought it back from California in the 1930s and kept it in Maine in a garage for a long, long time. The board was coming apart when he found it, and Mazza had to re-glue it. He speculated that the board is from the early 1930s, since the glue was not waterproof. "Another interesting thing is that it had the remnants of a deck pad made out of an old rubber bathtub mat held on by two strips of wood. You can see where the pad was on the deck because there is a rectangle of virgin varnish where the pad was. Probably the earliest pad on a board there is. The board shows a lot of craftsmanship and was obviously made by a professional wood worker." The board is very heavy because it is made of redwood and spruce. It has perfectly square rails.

Photos by Lucia Griggi; Boards courtesy John Mazza

13' Malloy Kookbox

On a cold but perfect winter day in Central California—when the sky was as blue as the hills were green—Chris Malloy shook off a fresh-busted rib to stand with a 13-foot kookbox replica. The board was put together by Mike Malloy, with help from his sons Chris, Keith, and Dan, on his scenic J2 Ranch. According to Chris, they made the board "just because we had a big interest in [Tom] Blake and wanted to see how those boards felt under our feet. And they do have some magic to them. We basically got our hands on a copy of the Blake plans from that old *Popular Mechanics*."

Their nouveau kookbox is 13 feet of marine-grade plywood and scrap 1x3s, "with maybe a stripped down two-by-four here and there," Chris added. The board emerged from the barns and sheds of the J2 Ranch in about 2006, but it wasn't a show horse—it was meant to be ridden hard and put away wet. Chris said that "with a stiff northeast wind [the board] really comes to life. When that offshore wind gets under your hull it takes all the weight out of them. The bottom becomes half wing, half planing surface. It's the only time strong wind under your board makes the board perform better. I've never felt a sensation like that while surfing. I don't think people were using them that way in the 1930s and '40s from the images I've seen. But who knows?"

Photos by Lucia Griggi/Lensbaby

14′ 6″ Hollowed Redwood Paddleboard

Something old and something new. Something mangled and something beautiful. For the 2007 book *The Surfboard: Art, Style, Stoke*, Brazilian *fotografista* Juliana Morais worked hard to photograph all the boards in Fernando Aguerre's collection—and it wasn't easy. Here she stands with a 14-foot, 6-inch paddleboard from that collection. According to Fernando, this hollowed-out, solid-redwood racing paddleboard was constructed in the 1930s. It was purchased at a police auction by Harvey Toda, who used the board for competition before passing it on to his son. The board is extremely narrow and made from a solid slab of redwood. The body was hollowed out and decking applied to cut down on weight. The board was partly devoured by termites, but they didn't get to the brass drain plug.

Photos by Juliana Morais; Board courtesy Fernando Aguerre

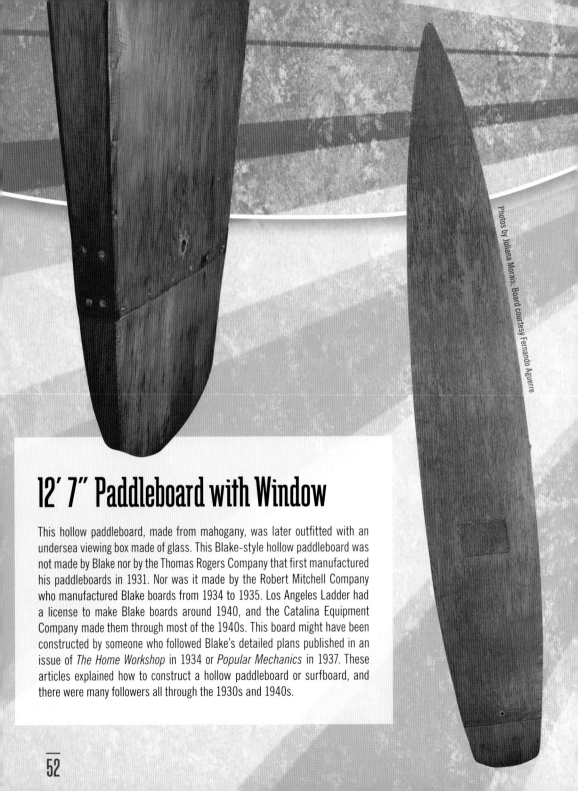

Photos by Juliana Morais; Board courtesy Fernando Aguerre

12′ 7″ Paddleboard with Window

This hollow paddleboard, made from mahogany, was later outfitted with an undersea viewing box made of glass. This Blake-style hollow paddleboard was not made by Blake nor by the Thomas Rogers Company that first manufactured his paddleboards in 1931. Nor was it made by the Robert Mitchell Company who manufactured Blake boards from 1934 to 1935. Los Angeles Ladder had a license to make Blake boards around 1940, and the Catalina Equipment Company made them through most of the 1940s. This board might have been constructed by someone who followed Blake's detailed plans published in an issue of *The Home Workshop* in 1934 or *Popular Mechanics* in 1937. These articles explained how to construct a hollow paddleboard or surfboard, and there were many followers all through the 1930s and 1940s.

Photo by Juliana Morais; Board courtesy Fernando Aguerre

9' 4" Aquaglider

This light metal, 9-foot, 4-inch Aquaglider board was designed/made by somebody named "Taylor" during the era of the wooden kookbox paddleboards. This Aquaglider is an early experiment in alternative materials. The bottom is made of channeled tin and is riveted to the deck of solid plywood, making it much lighter than the plywood and redwood boards. The board originally belonged to Gerhart "G" Stangeland and then it went to his son, Gary "the Goose" Stangeland. His nephew Mike got the board from Gary in exchange for a fireman's badge he owned. Fernando Aguerre adopted the board from Mike Stangeland in 2005.

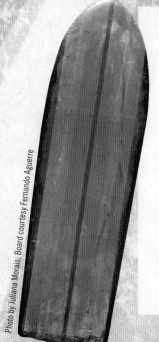

Photo by Juliana Morais; Board courtesy Fernando Aguerre

5' 1" Waikiki Bellyboard

This 5-foot, 1-inch Pacific Systems Homes Waikiki bellyboard was made after the rise of Nazism forced the company to change its brand from the Swastika to the Waikiki board. The boards were inspired by Hawaiian bellyboards, *alaia*, and planks, and they were popular in Hawaii. In the surfing version of taking coals to Newcastle, Meyers Butte shipped six Swastika boards to Hawaii in 1932. Far from getting laughed off the beach, the Swastika models became objects of desire at Waikiki. "The Swastika boards were droolers," Dale Velzy told Craig Stecyk. "Everybody had home-mades or hand-me-downs, so people really wanted a Pacific System. There were a lot of them around places where rich guys who had gotten them in Hawaii hung out, like the Bel Air Bay Club, the Jonathon Club, the Balboa Bay Club, and the Santa Monica Swim Club."

Scooter Boy Kaopuiki's 12' Kookbox

Tom Blake's *olo*-derived hollow paddleboards caused some stink in the Hawaiian Islands when they first started showing up there in the early 1930s. Some Hawaiians might have objected to a *haole* guy handling the *olo* boards of the Hawaiian monarchy—a centuries-old lineage that had been usurped by the Americans in 1896. Others thought the ultra-fast hollow paddleboards gave Blake an unfair advantage in competition—and they were right. But Blake's paddleboards soon caught on with the paddlers and surfers around Waikiki. Toward the end of the 1930s, beach boy Joseph "Scooter Boy" Kaopuiki was a common sight in the surf off Waikiki, riding waves on this 12-foot hollow board with his *poi* dog, Sandy. The board was Blake-style, but it was constructed by Funai boat builders, Japanese craftsmen based in Hawaii who constructed sampans for the Hawaiian fishing fleet before World War II. This big board had no skeg, and Scooter Boy was one of a few guys who could hotdog the board—getting past the length and the weight and the lack of a fin to hotdog it—with a dog on the nose.

Thomas Rogers Paddleboard

In addition to surfboards, the Thomas Rogers Company of Venice, California, also manufactured airplane wings, and a similar design is evident in the construction of this paddleboard. Like biplane wings, the board is hollow with a transversely braced (ribbed) interior. Designed by Tom Blake, the hollow surfboard significantly reduced the weight of solid-wood surfboards, making surfing accessible to a larger spectrum of people. Working closely with Rogers, Blake produced some of the earliest commercially manufactured surfboards and paddleboards. The latter were typically used by lifeguards or for racing but could also be used to ride waves. This paddleboard belonged to local Malibu lifeguard and surfer Bob Burns. On big-wave days, he used to throw it off the end of the Malibu Pier and paddle out from there.

14′ Swastika-turned-Waikiki Paddleboard

Look close at the Waikiki logo and you'll still see a hint of the swastika symbol that Pacific Systems Homes dropped in 1938 after Germany's National Socialist German Worker's Party adopted the symbol. This 14-foot paddleboard was used for racing and cruising but not surfing. Just as the Nazis ended the use of the swastika, the outbreak of World War II also ended the production of surfboards, as men and materials were turned toward war production, not frolicking in the surf. Waikiki boards were constructed in California, but the boards were popular along the beaches of Waikiki through the war and into the 1950s.

Board and photos courtesy John Mazza/Pepperdine University

5′ 11″ Waikiki Bellyboard

This Pacific Systems Homes Waikiki model bellyboard from the 1940s is constructed of balsa and redwood. The 5-foot, 11-inch board has a nose rocker to avoid pearling. Riding waves became more and more popular during World War II, as tens of thousands of young Americans shipped out to Hawaii and elsewhere in the South Pacific and saw people riding waves from Waikiki to Papua New Guinea to Sumatra. Some were happy just to ride bellyboards, and Pacific Systems Homes provided quality boards to the growing market.

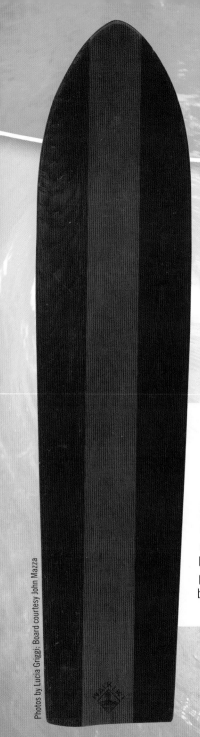

5′ 11″ Waikiki Steam Nose

This 5-foot, 11-inch Pacific Systems Homes Waikiki Steam Nose was offered for sale at the 2011 Hawaiian Islands Vintage Surf Auction. They gave the date of this thin, small surfboard as 1946 and explained that the Steam Nose name came from the process used to put a curve in the nose to help prevent the board from pearling. "The nose was saw-cut 18 inches from the nose and a piece glued in and steam-heated to allow for the nose rocker to be bent into the board. Redwood and pine construction with shellac finish."

11′ 8″ Tom Blake Catalina Model

This 11-foot, 8-inch hollow paddleboard still has the original drainage plug, although it is difficult to see who was the manufacturer of the plug. According to the Stoked 'n Board website, Thomas Rogers used a cast brass drain plug on boards from 1940 to 1941. Los Angeles Ladder also used a cast brass plug on the boards they made from the late 1940s to the early 1950s. The board also appears to have the word "Catalina" across the deck, which means this hollow paddleboard was manufactured by the Catalina Equipment Company sometime in the late 1940s or early 1950s.

Courtesy © Croul Publications

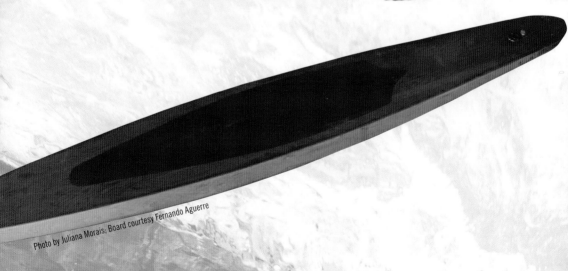

Photo by Juliana Morais; Board courtesy Fernando Aguerre

Blake Paddleboard by Catalina

The Catalina Equipment Company licensed the rights to make Tom Blake hollow paddleboards from the late 1940s into the 1950s. This board is 11 feet, 8 inches long by 23 inches wide and was made of marine plywood and another unknown wood. It is a classic example of Blake's square-railed paddleboard design.

Board and photos, courtesy Jimmy Buffett/Honolulu Surfing Museum

Mahogany Tom Blake Hollow Board

The glamorous mahogany wood can weigh anywhere from 31 to 53 pounds per cubic foot, depending on whether it's African, Cuban, Honduran, or Spanish mahogany. Compare that to 28 pounds for American redwood, and 7 to 9 pounds for balsa. But mahogany is gorgeous, and there is a lot of lovely hardwood in this 13-foot, 10-inch by 23-inch Tom Blake–style hollow wave-riding board made by the Catalina Equipment Company. Blake made different boards for paddling and for surfing: the surfboards had wider, square tails, ranged in size from 10 to 14 feet, and weighed mostly around 45 to 55 pounds. This board is inscribed with the Hawaiian word for wave (*nalu*) and has a semi-rounded rail that would have made it somewhat easier to turn and more forgiving of minor lapses in balance by the surfer.

According to Chris Dixon and Paul Holmes of the Honolulu Surfing Museum, "All of Blake's hollow boards featured what at first glance might look like a metal badge or emblem with the maker's company name. In fact, this feature is the seat of a screw-in brass plug, because no matter how well-made and maintained with varnish, the hollow boards were notoriously leaky and had to be taken ashore to be drained after every 20 or 30 minutes of use."

Board and photos courtesy Jimmy Buffett/Honolulu Surfing Museum

Tom Blake's First Fin

In Waikiki in the 1930s, Tom Blake was trying to figure out how to solve the problem of sliding ass. "When I first went to the Islands, they used wide-tailed boards, and they used to spinout on a steep, critical, slide," Blake said. "I figured it would be easy to correct that problem. Just add something—a keel." He looked to boats for his solution, as was detailed by Margaret Bairos in the *Honolulu Advertiser* in 1936. "My new hollow board is especially adapted for big waves," Blake was quoted in the article. "It weighs 116 pounds; and in huge 30-foot waves, the metal handle at the stern end of the board allows a surfer to hold it in a break. The most recent development is the attaching of a stabilizer or fin at the bottom of the board at the stern. I got the idea from airships. It helps to steer or control the board."

Blake was inspired by stabilizers on airships, but his first skeg came off a wrecked motorboat, an aluminum piece that was 4 inches deep and 6 inches long. It was too pitted and sharp to leave unexposed, so Blake put a piece of koa wood over the fin before attaching it to a 14-foot paddleboard. The first time he paddled it, all that directional stability felt weird, and he thought it was a bogus idea and considered discarding it. Then, as he recalled, "I took it out and caught a pretty good wave on it, a six-foot wave, maybe, and it was remarkable the control you had over the board with this little skeg on it. It didn't spin out, it steered easy, because the tail held steady when you put the pressure on the front, and it turned any way you wanted it, and I knew right from that moment it was a success." Strangely, it took another 10 years for the skeg to catch on with more surfers, but that's how the surfing world is—skegs, wetsuits, and surf leashes all took time to be accepted.

Photos by John Clark

Hawaii resident and author John Clark sent photos of these holy relics from surf history: early examples of Blake's fins. According to legendary surfer Wally Froiseth, Blake made three aluminum skegs at the old Honolulu Ironworks and gave one to Gene "Tarzan" Smith, one to Froiseth, and kept one for himself. In September 2012, Clark visited Froiseth, who still had the fin Tom gave him. It measures 7 inches long, has a 1⅝-inch-wide base, and a 2-inch-high blade.

Courtesy © Croul Publications

George Downing's Pepe Hot Curl

Photo by Greg Lui-Kwan

In 2010, *Surfer* magazine ranked George Downing 42nd on the list of the 50 Most Important Surfers of All Time. Christian Beamish—who called Downing a pioneer of big-wave riding and a key contributor to design innovations that "broke the barrier to 20-foot surf and beyond"—described one of Downing's early projects in which he shaped a redwood plank into a more maneuverable "hot curl" design. This was in Waikiki in 1943, and he worked with Wally Froiseth on the project. Downing dubbed the board "Pepe" and rode it all over the South and North Shores of Oahu, noting its amazing speed. "By changing the vee through the tail section to a semi-round shape," Beamish explained, "Downing was able to run a flatter bottom forward, and found what he referred to as 'the board of my dreams.' . . . The lessons he learned in altering the tail section of Pepe would lead to experiments with skegs (including the creation of a fin box) that would transform notions of what was possible on a surfboard."

Photo by Mark Cane; Board courtesy Marc Andreini.

Marc Andreini's Redwood Hot Curl

Marc Andreini's 10-foot, 8-inch-long by 3-inch-thick hot curl replica is made of redwood, and it's as heavy (82 pounds) as it is pretty. He made the board for a San Francisco fireman named Mark Cane. "His cousin scored a solid slab of redwood topped from a 1,300-year-old tree," Andreini said. "Details cannot be revealed! He brought me the slab in 2011 and I replicated probably the most beautiful of all surfboard designs." The board was modeled after hot curls from the mid-1920s. "This finless straight-rocker stiletto gives the ultimate glide to those who master it." Andreini says that most shapers at some point revisit ancient and early finless designs. "I have made at least 18 of them and surfed two during a one-year period. This board is surfable but is hanging on the wall for now!"

10' PSH Waikiki with a Skeg

This Pacific Systems Homes Waikiki model was retrofitted with a skeg in the late 1930s when they came in vogue. The 10-foot-long, balsa-and-redwood board has never been restored and is of typical shape for the planks of the era. Although Pacific Systems Homes boards were made on the mainland, they were very popular in Hawaii.

These boards often appeared in photographs and movies, and the Bishop Museum is home to many hours of moving images of surfing, beginning with a 1906 Thomas Edison "actuality" of surf riders at Waikiki Beach and continuing up through World War II. There are home movies, tourist movies, all kinds of movies that show surf riding at Waikiki, inevitably with the broad shoulders of Diamond Head in the background. In all those movies, much of the surfing is being done straight in—looks like fun, but not much angling. That begins to change in the 1930s as the use of hot curls and skegs allowed surfers to angle and even start to hotdog a little.

1937 Redwood Hot Curl

This 10-foot, 8-inch redwood hot curl was made around 1937 and shows how the modern surfboard shape began to evolve during this period. A classic example of the redwood hot curl era, the board has clean template lines and well-transitioned foils. The tail is pulled in to accommodate Hawaii's hollow surf. Holes were drilled to attach a rope, for ease in holding on to the board. Originally owned by a Hawaiian family in the Kalihi Valley, this hot curl was ridden in Waikiki until the mid-1950s and was most likely surfed by the Duke at that time. It was later left in the family's backyard.

Three Wood Hot Curl

This 10-foot, 3-inch hot curl is made of redwood, balsa, and pine. It most likely started life as a Pacific Systems Homes square-tail, and at some point, someone took tools to the tail and pulled the rails in from a straight line to make a board that wouldn't slide ass. The board was owned and surfed by John Blyth around Oahu, primarily at the breaks at Waikiki and Makaha.

10' 5" Authentic Swastika Model

This 10-foot, 5-inch Swastika model from Pacific Systems Homes is the real deal, according to owner Griff Snyder. Because swastikas were not exactly a popular symbol in the late 1930s, many of the original Swastika boards had the symbol altered or destroyed. By the end of the 20th century, however, the rarity of original, unaltered boards made them desired and valuable, and many boards have re-created swastikas on them. Snyder's research, done for an article in *The Surfer's Journal*, convinced him that this was an original. "We looked really hard and found three real Swastika boards for publication," Snyder said, "and maybe there are ten more out there still in existence." This George "Firehose" Feister board is genuine, and Snyder first saw it in Feister's garage over 40 years ago in its original state. "This was before anyone cared about old wood surfboards, and surf Nazis were an embarrassment from the 1950s. The indisputable documentation came from Leroy Grannis's Palos Verdes Surf Club archives, which contain a picture of Feister as a lad in 1937 with the board—the Swastika clearly visible in the photo." According to Snyder, Feister added the oak-wood fin in the late 1930s.

Photos by Lucia Griggi; Board courtesy Griff Snyder

Balsa Board with Skeg

This 9-foot, 10-inch balsa board, with skeg, wrapped in airplane fiberglass dates from the late 1940s or early 1950s. This board wasn't made by any of the big names of the time—Joe Quigg, Matt Kivlin, Bob Simmons—but the length and shape were clearly inspired by what those guys were doing in the back alleys of Santa Monica and Venice—and even in the garage of California Governor and Chief Justice of the Supreme Court Earl Warren, whose daughter "Honey Bear" was part of the surfer crowd.

Photos by Juliana Morais; Board courtesy Fernando Aguerre

Bob Simmons
Channeled Balsa

This 10-foot, dual-finned, channeled balsa was built in about 1949 by Bob Simmons, one of the heads on the Mount Rushmore of surfboard design. After dropping out of Cal Tech in the early 1940s, Simmons put his sophisticated education and natural love for hydrodynamics to use by bringing science to surfing. Through the 1940s and early 1950s, he applied Bernoulli's principle of fluid dynamics and planing hull technology to building surfboards. He experimented with "scarfed noses," channels, twin fins, balsa wood, and then foam and fiberglass.

Simmons was born and raised in Southern California, and a bicycle accident when he was a teenager left him with a permanently crippled elbow. While in the hospital, a patient suggested that Simmons try surfing. He got his first board in 1939—when boards were either solid wood planks or Tom Blake hollow paddleboards. Either way, they weighed a lot for a kid with a crook elbow, and his disability would mother his innovation. His innovations still resonate, 60 years later.

Tragically, Simmons drowned while surfing a big south swell near Windansea in September 1954.

Nohea and Jetboard

Before the Internet, Griff Snyder realized that the surfing equivalent of Babe Ruth's baseball bat and Ty Cobb's cleats were stuck in garages and rafters all around Southern California. Griff put an ad in the *Los Angeles Times* classifieds: "OLD WOOD SURFBOARDS = CASH $$$$$$$$$." That got him a lot of phone calls. He logged all of them, tracked down some, and found some classic surfboards, which he paid hundreds of dollars for and are now worth many thousands.

Standing in front of his beach home, Griff holds one of the prized boards in his collection. According to Griff, the board was made by "Big Dave" Rochlen back in 1948 and ridden at Malibu, around California, and at Waikiki. "It's the earliest gun-style board I can think of. There are hot curls that had a gun shape, but this is balsa and it has a fin." It is branded with the word *nohea*, which is Hawaiian for "comely" or "good looking."

Within Griff's massive home is a rumpus room with a window looking into his swimming pool. Above that window is an all-aluminum Jetboard, one of many that were produced during the mid-1960s and sold for a whopping $1,700—the equivalent of about $10,200 in modern dollars. The Jetboard had a 6.25 HP Tecumseh engine that powered a jet pump made by Jacuzzi. The board had a kill switch and other high techery of the day.

Photos by Lucia Griggi/Lensbaby

9′ 6″ Bob Simmons Balsa

Sometimes what looks crude and clunky in the 21st century was state of the art in the 1950s. This 9-foot, 6-inch Bob Simmons balsa was a Ferrari compared to the Pacific Systems Homes hardwoods and big plank jalopies of only a few years before. It was 2 feet shorter and as much as 80 pounds lighter. The big fin slotted all the way back in the tail kept all that speed from sliding ass.

Photos by Juliana Morais; Board courtesy Fernando Aguerre

Joe Quigg's Malibu Chip

According to Matt Warshaw's *History of Surfing*, the Malibu Chip evolved from "girl boards" Joe Quigg first made for Darrylin Zanuck around 1947 and then for Aggie Bane and Vicki Flaxman, while Matt Kivlin made boards for Robin Grigg, Diane Griffith, and Claire Cassidy. "The boards were all about 9 feet long," wrote Warshaw, "with more rocker and a narrower profile than the still-circulating Darrylin 10-footer, and by carefully picking only the lightest balsa, Quigg and Kivlin trimmed the weight down to 25 pounds."

Photo by Juliana Morais; Board courtesy Fernando Aguerre

1950 Malibu Chip

Shaun Tomson in 1975 and Kelly Slater in 1992 both rode slender boards that were called "potato ships," but the original "potato chip" goes back to this 9-foot, 4-inch by 23-inch balsa board wrapped in fiberglass. The boards, which were made for the growing number of female surfers at Malibu, were designed by Joe Quigg. "It helped the girls to leave the tails wide," recalled Quigg. "I'd put what I called easy-rider rocker in them. They were real easy to ride. A lot of girls learned how to surf on those boards in just a few months."

According to Paul Holmes and Chris Dixon of the Honolulu Surfing Museum, a group of Malibu surfers traveled to San Diego's Windansea for a Fourth of July weekend surfing contest in 1950 and brought these new boards with them. Quigg recalled that a local guy, Art Cunningham, saw the curvy, yellowish boards and noted, "Wow, look at those potato chips!"

"Known thereafter as Malibu Chips," continued Holmes and Dixon, "the balsa and fiberglass boards were a milestone in board design and a turning point in the evolution of surfing performance."

Hot Curl + Balsa Chip

This 9-foot, 4-inch balsa board is a combination of hot curl with balsa chip, bringing speed and turnability with directional stability. Before, during, and after World War II, a lot of California surfers traveled to Hawaii and saw great surfers cutting great angles and shooting the curl at Waikiki. They could ride high and do turns, all without fins, and the Californians wanted to do the same at their point breaks and beachbreaks. This board has a wider tail and less vee to suit California waves, which are generally not as fast or powerful as Hawaiian waves. The logo was probably added when the board was restored, as most balsa boards were undecorated because balsa grain was considered too lovely to cover up.

1950s Bob Simmons Slot

Just as surfers in the 1930s had a problem with skegless surfboards sliding ass and spinning out, surfers in the 1940s and 1950s had problems with the noses of their boards submerging and "pearling"—causing a wipeout. Bob Simmons's solutions to this problem included "scarfed noses" and "the Slot." This 8-foot, 8-inch Simmons Slot is from the early 1950s. The theory behind the slot nose was to redirect water flow from the bottom to the deck, because less wetted surface means more speed. The concept didn't work as well as Simmons might have wanted, but this board is one example of his innovation and experimentation and shows how far ahead of the pack he was in the 1950s. Greg Noll, who came along in the generation following Simmons, noted in his book, *Greg Noll: The Art of the Surfboard*, that Simmons was "thinking about things no one else was considering. . . . Concaves, double fins, first guy that applied fiberglass to balsa wood boards."

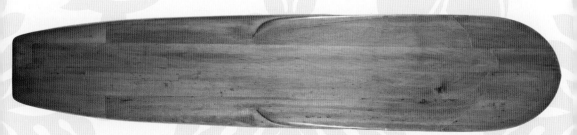

1951 Dale Velzy
9′ 4″ "Rope Logo" Board

What looks to be a foam and fiberglass 1960s board with yellow tint has a Hollywood back story longer than its 9-foot, 4-inch length. The board was shaped by celebrated Southern California board-maker Dale Velzy and came to the John Mazza collection at Pepperdine University from the 2009 Hawaiian Islands Vintage Surf Auction. It was one of Velzy's "rope logo" balsa boards. According to the Stoked-n-Board website, curated by Andy Anderson, Velzy used that logo on no more than 25 boards between 1950 and 1954.

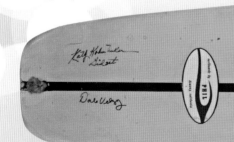

Board and photos courtesy John Mazza/Pepperdine University

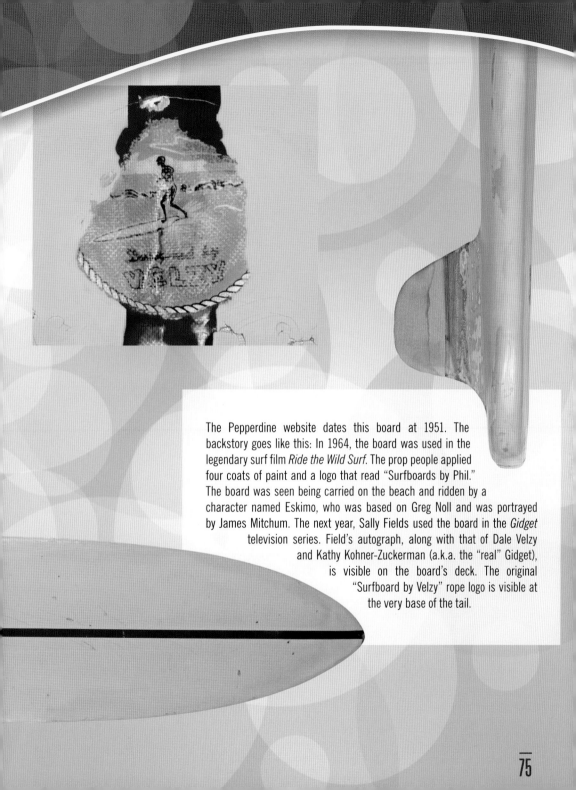

The Pepperdine website dates this board at 1951. The backstory goes like this: In 1964, the board was used in the legendary surf film *Ride the Wild Surf*. The prop people applied four coats of paint and a logo that read "Surfboards by Phil." The board was seen being carried on the beach and ridden by a character named Eskimo, who was based on Greg Noll and was portrayed by James Mitchum. The next year, Sally Fields used the board in the *Gidget* television series. Field's autograph, along with that of Dale Velzy and Kathy Kohner-Zuckerman (a.k.a. the "real" Gidget), is visible on the board's deck. The original "Surfboard by Velzy" rope logo is visible at the very base of the tail.

Otis Chandler's Simmons Balsa

Two of the greatest surfboard shapers of all time laid their hands to this 10-foot, 10-inch by 22½-inch balsa and redwood plank. The board was originally made by Pete Peterson in the 1930s and was once owned by Otis Chandler, a member of a surfing family who also founded and published the *Los Angeles Times* from 1960 to 1978. Before Chandler, the board belonged to a Hollywood stockbroker, writer, actor, director, and producer named Bob Brant. Chandler acquired the board after he began dating and subsequently married Brant's sister, Marilyn "Missy" Brant, in 1950.

This Pacific Systems Homes board had a domed bottom but very little rocker or kick in the nose. Chandler had a problem with pearling—a dangerous thing with a big, hardwood board that could hit you in the head or break your ribs—so he took it to Bob Simmons, who added a redwood extension to the board's nose to give it a more forgiving flip. This technique was called "scarfing" the nose, which according to the Honolulu Surfing Museum website involves "cutting across the board's nose at an angle, glue-and-doweling an additional section of wood, and then reshaping the area to blend in the curves. A fiberglass patch was often used to add strength and integrity to the job."

10′ 6″ Bob Simmons Painted Balsa

Most balsa surfboards were made from planks of balsa that were glued together then shaped. In 1954, Bob Simmons shaped this 10-foot, 6-inch board out of a solid piece of balsa wood. It was built for Coronado lifeguard Wayne Tompkins.

Woody Brown's 1953 Balsa Board

According to John Mazza, this 10-foot, 2-inch balsa board was custom-made for Woody Brown by Woody Brown, who rode it at Makaha during the early 1950s. Woody wasn't too keen on Tom Blake's skegs originally, but eventually he came around to understand their function. Woody would go on to bring the double-hulled canoe into the modern world. Every catamaran you see on the water goes back to him. Unfortunately, he never patented his designs for these first modern catamarans; he just wanted to make boats he could use to sail tourists off the beach at Waikiki and support his family. Had he patented his designs, he would have been richer than Hobart "Hobie" Alter. But Woody was born rich, didn't like it, and preferred a simple life of the sun and the sea and the wind.

1953 Dale Velzy Pig

Dale Velzy wasn't head over heels for the Malibu Chips being ridden by a lot of guys up the coast from the South Bay. He had his own ideas on how to make surfboards more maneuverable, and in 1953, he reversed the typical shape of a surfboard to make one that was little in the middle but had much back. That is, the board was narrow in the nose and wide in the hips—not pretty, but it worked. Velzy rode the board at Hermosa Beach in 1953, and soon the likes of Hap Jacobs, Mickey Munoz, Miki Dora, Mike Doyle, and other hot guys were turning and burning on a board that was christened the Pig. The shape of the board resonated through the 1960s and up to now, as the wide point moved back for turning and burning and noses stayed thin.

Photos by Juliana Morais; Board courtesy Fernando Aguerre.

Photo by Joe Curren

Pulse on a Velzy Pig

Well-traveled Oregonian artist Spencer Reynolds painted this piece of art, which he calls *Pulse*, on a Donald Takayama replica of a Velzy Pig. According to Reynolds, the board belonged to a collector and friend of Donald Takayama that he met in Santa Barbara—who trusted a stranger to take a valuable board back to Oregon. "I don't paint many surfboards," Reynolds said, "and was really nervous to paint this one. . . . The raw ocean wave is juxtaposed against the clean lines and beautiful craftsmanship of the surfboard. I named it *Pulse* as an afterthought when I noticed the pinstripe highlights on the wave-face look like an EKG reading."

Photo by Lucia Griggi; Board courtesy Tom Moore

Tom Moore's
Long-Lost Kivlin Balsa

Tom Moore stands with a 10-foot, 6-inch tinted balsa gun made by Matt Kivlin. This board has a long story, beginning with Moore's first trip to Hawaii in 1952 where he found that his 9-foot, 6-inch Simmons board with a 17-inch tail couldn't handle the bowl at Makaha. In the summer of 1954, Kivlin agreed to make a 10-foot, 6-inch balsa board for Moore, which Moore rode on the North Shore and Makaha and then took to Australia in 1956 to compete in the Olympic International Surf Carnival at Torquay Beach, Victoria.

In December 1957, Moore was through with school, and before he returned to California, he sold the board to Joe Gilman for $50. Forty years later Moore found out that the board was still alive and well and he made a deal to buy it back.

"We went back and forth for a year," Moore recalled, "and the price went to $1,500 and then $2,000, and then I called him and said, 'You and I aren't going to be around much longer, and I would like to keep it in the family and give it to my son Tommy.' I offered Joe $5,000 for it. He said, 'I can't turn that down,' so I flew to Hawaii and gave him a check for $5,000." The board was in almost perfect shape. Back in California, an appraiser from the Surfing Heritage and Cultural Center checked out the board and appraised it at 95 percent. "I've had offers of close to $50,000," Moore said. "Not for sale."

In August 2009, Moore attended a memorial service for long-time Malibu surfer Dusty Peak. "There were a thousand people on the beach and that Kivlin balsa attracted a lot of attention. I took it out and caught a wave and then my son Tommy wanted to test it out. I said, 'This board is 52 years old, it weighs 45 pounds and it doesn't have a leash.' But Tommy took it out and caught a half dozen waves and rode it fine. Didn't lose it. Still no dings."

1955 Velzy-Jacobs

John Mazza's 9-foot, 6-inch board from 1955 is a very early example of a Velzy-Jacobs creation, judging by the placement of the fin—which also has a rare Velzy-Jacobs sticker on it. Dale Velzy and Hap Jacobs first got together in 1954 to open Velzy-Jacobs Surfboards, where they built mostly solid balsa wood boards with fiberglass skin. According to Mazza, "Velzy was the master promoter, and so from the mid-1950s through the mid-1960s, his boards and shops enjoyed 'top of the heap' status. Velzy Surfboards or Velzy-Jacobs was the board every fledgling surf kid wanted." By the end of the decade, Velzy-Jacobs had about half a dozen shops throughout Southern California and Hawaii.

Photos by Lucia Griggi; Board courtesy John Mazza

9' 8" Gordon Duane Balsa Board

Straight outta Compton, this 9-foot, 8-inch balsa board was made by Gordon "Gordie" Duane. Gordie began surfing in Hawaii in 1951 at the age of 21 while he was stationed at Pearl Harbor. Returning to Southern California, Gordie shaped boards out of his parents' house in Lynwood, which is close to South Gate and Compton. Duane opened Gordie Surfboards in Huntington Beach in 1956, so this board with "Compton" on the label is pre-1956 and an extremely rare specimen from Gordie's early shaping career. This board has been featured in several coffee table books and has been seen in several magazines.

Photos by Lucia Griggi; Board courtesy Griff Snyder

Malibu Chip Signed By Gidget

This 9-foot, 10-inch by 22-inch balsa Malibu Chip was signed "To SBSM" (Santa Barbara Surf Museum) by one of the biggest cultural icons of the mid-1950s: Kathy "Gidget" Kohner.

This board was made in the 1950s, around the same time that Kohner began surfing the beaches of Malibu. Ten years earlier, surfboards were made of redwood and weighed a hundred pounds, which was heavier than a girl like Kathy, and most female surfers rode tandem with guys who could carry the boards. A light balsa and fiberglass Malibu Chip board like this one is the kind that Kathy used in her initiation to the secrets of the sea. She could stick it in the back of a convertible car and carry it down to the beach without help. Kohner would be labeled with the nickname Gidget ("girl" + "midget") and a cultural icon was born—thanks to her screenwriter father, Frederick Kohner, who recorded her tales of riding the waves and hanging out with the colorful crew at Malibu. In 1957 the elder Kohner put these stories together in a fictionalized novella called *Gidget: The Little Girl with Big Ideas*, which went on to sell half a million copies.

Board and photos courtesy Jimmy Buffett/Honolulu Surfing Museum

1950s French Plankys

There are great waves along the French Atlantic Coast, from the Spanish border up to the English Channel, and French surfers rode waves standing up and lying down. According to Philip Zibin, Frenchman Jacques "Jacky" Rott (pictured here) was a cabinetmaker from Dax, France, who made wooden bellyboards—known as plankys—in the 1950s. The blue board is Rott's personal board from that time, and the other board is the original template, which has never been in the water. The five-ply boards were made in a press, and originally the boards were flat. The nose lift has been attributed to another local of Biarritz, France: inventor Georges Hennebutte.

Spain also has great waves from the French border to Portugal, and the Spanish version of this bellyboard was known as *txampero* (a gadget to take advantage of the strength of a wave) around San Sebastian; *planquin* in Cantabria; or *corre olas* (wave runner) in Asturias.

Australian *paipo* scholar Bob Green credits Rott with making the first fiberglassed balsa board in France. "He went on to form a partnership with Michel Barland, who established the first commercial surfboard factory in France. From the Barland-Rott factory, surfboards were sent all over Europe."

Colonel Churchstone's Kookbox

By the middle 1950s, the Sport of Kings had spread all the way to the Sceptered Isle. According to Alex Williams and Alasdair Lindsey, this board was made from a single sheet of 8-foot by 4-foot plywood and measures out at 8 feet long and 24 inches wide, with pine rails. Williams points out that the lack of knots in the plywood and pine is indicative of the board's age; more recent plywood from the 1960s has many more knots in the wood. This board belonged to Lt. Col. Mikalia Churchstone, who learned to surf with the Americans during or shortly after World War II on Okinawa Island. Upon coming home to England, he looked up and down the Cornish and Devon coast for a board, but he couldn't find one. So he had this one made, or perhaps made it himself. Colonel Churchstone's board was seen being surfed at Bantham in South Devon in the 1960s.

1956 Clean Hobie Balsa

Born in 1933, Hobart "Hobie" Alter was a cool surfer dude and a woodshop geek at the same time. He divided his time between the family home in the Inland Empire and a beach home in Laguna Beach. In the summer of 1950, Hobie persuaded his dad to move the family Desoto out of the garage of the beach house, and that was where Hobie began crafting balsa wood surfboards. "I started out making maybe 20 boards a summer for my friends," Hobie explained to Laura Bly of the *Santa Ana Daily Register*, "and it sure beat being a lifeguard. About the end of junior college—which took me a little longer because I was doing a lot of surfing and skiing—my father decided I'd learned everything I could, and he recommended I go into the board business full time."

Hobie made 99 boards in his garage but saved number 100 until he opened his first shop at Dana Point in 1953. His production went from 99 boards to 1,580 balsas, all but two of them hand-shaped by Hobie. This 9-foot, 9-inch board was made in 1956, about two years after Hobie began experimenting with polyurethane foam and fiberglass.

Board and photos courtesy John Mazza/Pepperdine University

HAWAIIAN
PAI PO
BOARD

Mfg. By
FROISETH

Photo by John Clark

The Origins of *Paipo*

The origin of the term *paipo* is wrapped in some mystery, but *paipo* aficionado Rod Rodgers cites John R. K. Clark's explanation in *Hawaiian Surfing* that shortboards under 6 feet in length were referred to as *papa li'ili'i* (small boards) in ancient Hawaii. By the early 1900s, according to Clark, non-Hawaiian surfers began calling them bellyboards, since they were often ridden with the rider lying on his or her stomach. In addition, explained Clark, "Hawaiian surfers in Waikiki called them *pae po'o* boards. The literal translation of *pae po'o* is 'ride [a wave] head-first,' or in other words, bodysurf, and a *papa pae po'o* was a bodysurfing board, or what surfers today call a bodyboard."

The word *paipo* comes from Wally Froiseth, one of the founders of the hot curl and also a keen bellyboarder. Seeing a market for the boards in Hawaii and overseas, Froiseth made approximately 150 *paipo* boards from 1956 to 1986, and he sold them to friends and other surfers. He branded his boards with decals bearing a word that he had heard spoken but never seen in print, so he called them "pai po." The decals read, "Hawaiian Pai Po Board. Mfg. by Froiseth." "Pai po" morphed into "paipo," and in Froiseth's wake, several manufacturers adopted the term in their company names, such as Paipo Nui, El Paipo, Newport Paipo, and House of Paipo.

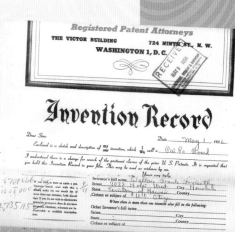

Velzy-Jacobs Bellyboard

Dale Velzy and Hap Jacobs made a few bodyboards out of balsa—for those who liked to ride on their bellies or who were working their way up to a regular surfboard. It is possible this board was made for Dale Velzy's son, Matt, when he was a child.

1956 Catalina Cruiser

This photo shows Tom Zahn in 1956 holding an 18-foot, 8-inch-long by 17½-inch-wide, 23-pound hollow, balsa-ribbed paddleboard with aluminum rudder and foot tiller. The photo was taken by Tom Blake and bears this inscription on the back: "Tom Zahn – San Onofre – 4 mi paddleboard race. 1956. Zahn 3rd, Bones Bright first, Hobie Alter 2d. Zahn too thin. Pic. By Tom Blake"

Courtesy Gary Lynch and Joe Quigg

The board, which now hangs on the wall of Spencer Croul's office, was designed by Joe Quigg and, according to Croul, was made for Quigg himself to race from Two Harbors in Catalina to Manhattan Beach in the second annual Catalina paddleboard race; he placed third. "So," Croul explains, "he put the word 'Catalina' on the deck. He raced it only twice and sold it to Tom Zahn, who went on to set the record on it in 1958. Zahn's record on that board held for many years." The board was beautifully restored by Carl Ekstrom for Roy Bream, who owned and paddled it before Croul.

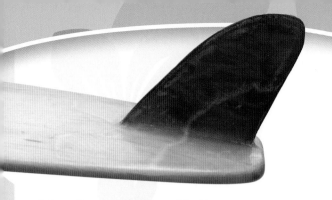

The Cop's Velzy Balsa

Dale Velzy was one of the first surfboard manufacturers to label his boards with stickers, and one of the first to own a surf shop in California. In the 1950s, a Venice cop saw someone breaking into Velzy's shop along the beach in Venice. He arrested the thief and most likely saved Velzy a lot of money. Velzy thanked the flatfoot by making him a perfect 10-foot, 6-inch balsa board—the finest board available at the time. The cop rode it once, didn't like surfing, and put it in his rafters in Glendale where Griff Snyder found it, around 40 years later, covered in a layer of dust and a dead rat. The board was ridden once and is in almost flawless condition.

Photos by Lucia Griggi; Board courtesy Griff Snyder

Tally Ho's Twelver

Hard to tell without scale, but this is a *huge* balsa board: 12 feet long, 25 inches wide, and 4 inches thick. It was custom made for a huge man and is one of John Mazza's sentimental favorites, which he obtained at a 2011 auction. "I grew up in LA and remember Lord Blears as a wrestler at the Olympic Stadium and saw him many times," Mazza recalled. "That of course predates all his surfing history and his son and daughter's surfing prominence."

Who is this guy, Lord Blears? A 1950s version of Lord Ted Deerhurst? Another randy member of the British aristocracy who became a surf bum? Not quite. Lord James "Tally Ho" Blears was a British-born wrestler who moved to Hawaii and became a prominent and colorful figure on the pro wrestling scene from the late 1940s until the mid-1960s. Two of his children had successful surfing careers: Jimmy Blears was the 1972 World Amateur Champion, and Laura Blears was a top female surfer in the 1970s and '80s.

Photo by Lucia Griggi; Board courtesy John Mazza

Bing Copeland's Tahitian Pig

Reunited and it feels so gooood. Bing Copeland left the Coast Guard in late 1957, and early in 1958 Dale Velzy made him this 9-foot, 4-inch-long, 22-inch-wide, 3¼-inch-thick Pig right before Copeland left for a trip to Tahiti and New Zealand. As Copeland tells it, "The photo of the yacht was taken by Bev Morgan when we were in Tahiti and just about to leave for New Zealand—where Rick Stoner and I introduced the modern surfboard to the Kiwis in late 1958." The board was later restored and preserved by the Piha Surf Club, where Copeland was reunited with it for a 50-year reunion in 2008. "Pretty cool if you ask me."

Photos courtesy Bing Copeland and Bev Morgan

Photo by Scott E. Linnenkohl

Rosemari Rice's 9' Quigg Balsa

Rosemari Russell started surfing in 1954 in her hometown of Hermosa Beach. Her first board was made in 1954 by Johnny Rice when he was working for Dale Velzy. "All balsa and dark blue with my name in yellow at the tip—all in the resin," Rosemari said with a sigh. "I wish I still had the board."

Courtesy Rosemari Rice

Rosemari does still have a 9-foot-long by 23-inch-wide balsa board that was shaped by Joe Quigg and glassed by Sonny Vardeman. She got the board in 1957 and rode it until around 1962, when the world switched to foam and fiberglass, and Rosemari switched with it—riding a 9-foot, 6-inch for Bing Copeland and a 9-foot to 9-foot, 6-inch for Dewey Weber. In 1970 Rosemari moved to Santa Cruz and has lived there ever since in a cool little hippie beach bungalow. Rosemari lives in the house with Rice, whom she married in 1989. There are a lot of beautiful surfboards in that house—wood and plastic—but this is one of the best non-Johnnys.

Wingnut's Baby Balsa Replica

Robert "Wingnut" Weaver is the proud owner of a replica of Phil Edwards's beloved 1958 balsa "Baby," custom-made for him by Edwards himself for a tidy four-figure sum. The board measures 9 feet, 10¾ inches long by 22 inches wide by 3 inches thick. Wingnut rides it in the point breaks of Santa Cruz, and he likes the life of wood. "Phil shaped this board for me in 1994. . . . The balsa had been stashed in Phil's garage, and the planks were super clean and super light. Ron House of Surf Glass chambered the balsa, so it's very light—only 20 pounds.

The original California power surfer, Edwards always preferred wood boards, and he continued to use "Baby" long after most surfers had switched to foam. "We used to have a saying," he said in 1992: "Spastic on plastic, good on wood."

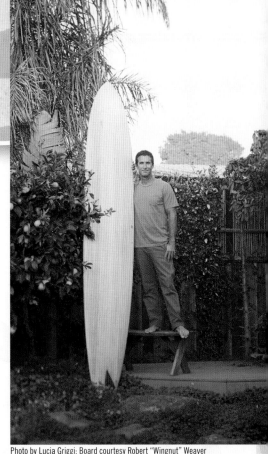

Photo by Lucia Griggi; Board courtesy Robert "Wingnut" Weaver

According to Wingnut, "If you want to see Baby in action, check out Bruce Brown's *Slippery When Wet* and watch Phil Edwards at Maili Point. . . . Baby was the board that Phil rode during his prime years in the balsa days and early foam days. The shape made the transition into the foam and fiberglass era and became the three-stringer Phil Edwards Model—the first signature-model board!"

Photo © Nikki Brooks

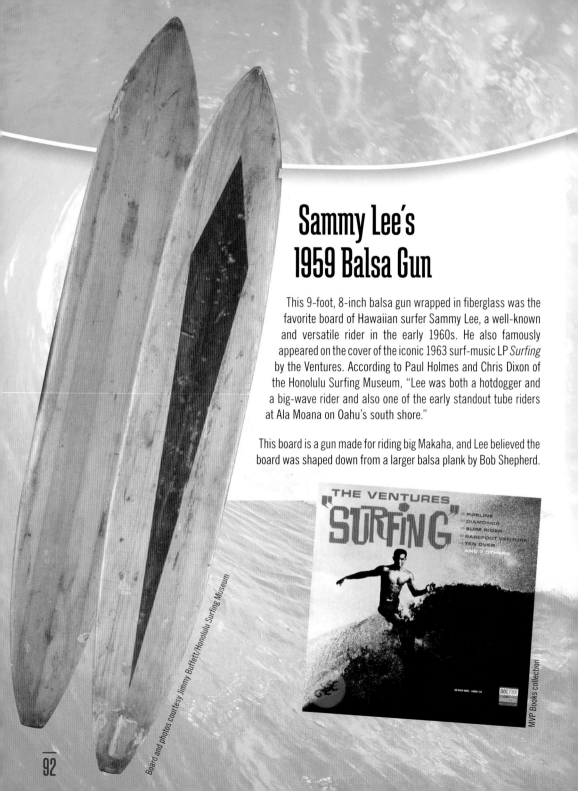

Sammy Lee's
1959 Balsa Gun

This 9-foot, 8-inch balsa gun wrapped in fiberglass was the favorite board of Hawaiian surfer Sammy Lee, a well-known and versatile rider in the early 1960s. He also famously appeared on the cover of the iconic 1963 surf-music LP *Surfing* by the Ventures. According to Paul Holmes and Chris Dixon of the Honolulu Surfing Museum, "Lee was both a hotdogger and a big-wave rider and also one of the early standout tube riders at Ala Moana on Oahu's south shore."

This board is a gun made for riding big Makaha, and Lee believed the board was shaped down from a larger balsa plank by Bob Shepherd.

Board and photos courtesy Jimmy Buffett/Honolulu Surfing Museum

MVP Books collection

Photo by Greg Lui-Mawaii

1950 George Downing's 10' Rocket

Most surfers wish they had saved all the boards in their life. George Downing has, going back to 1941. This 1950 Rocket is one of two 10-foot, 35-pound balsa guns that evolved from Downing's Pepe hot curl. George flattened the round bottom, which helped the board turn, but to address the problem of sliding ass, he took a fin from a water ski, screwed it to the bottom, and went to Makaha. "That was the first time I started to understand how," Downing recalled to *The Surfer's Journal* in 2005, "with skeg support of the stern, we could move forward in the development of flatter board bottoms."

Downing made this board to be ridden with a skeg, so he built a skeg box to move the fin around and experiment. Once the fin felt right, he glassed it in. "The biggest waves I ever rode were on this board—Sunset, Laniakea, Makaha Point," he said. "I had so much confidence in this board that I never felt, once I was trimming across and set into the face, that it could not make it to the end of the curl line. The Rocket allowed me to go fast enough to identify the dragging curves of rails and bottom rockers."

Luis Hangca's 1954 Balsa

Luis Hangca was a waterman and surfer who was a member of the Hawaiian team that surfed in an exhibition at a lifeguard competition in Melbourne, Australia, alongside the 1956 Olympic Games. That exhibition has gone down in history as the introduction of modern "Malibu" longboards to Australia. This board dates to 1954 and is a classic, 9-foot balsa gun made for big Hawaiian surf. The board sold for $3,500 at the 2003 Hawaiian Vintage Surf Auction.

Photos by Juliana Morais; Board courtesy Fernando Aguerre

10' 1" Hobie-Yater Balsa

Both Hobie Alter and Reynolds Yater left their mark on the tail of this 10-foot, 1-inch by 22-inch balsa gun. On the nose is some kind of religious medallion. Was this board used in pagan rituals to bring the surf up? According to Paul Holmes and Chris Dixon, Hobie was inspired to make this gun by a couple of George Downing Makaha guns brought back to California by Phillip "Flippy" Hoffman and Jim "Burrhead" Drever. Hobie was 21 at the time and made a series of Makaha guns, and this is one of the last remaining survivors. It was carefully restored with a balsa section in the tail and a mahogany fin. Yater glassed the board at Hobie's Dana Point workshop when it was first made. The medallion on the board is a Saint Christopher medal, a symbol for the patron saint and protector of travelers and seafarers. During the 1950s and early '60s, many surfers adopted the Saint Christopher medal as a symbol of their individuality and also for their safety.

1955 Surf Rat

The big-wave guns of the 1950s were all about the need for speed—but this? Jim O'Mahoney is the curator of the Santa Barbara Surf Museum and is responsible for many of the finer boards in this book. He sent these photos as this book was being finished, and they were hard to resist. But we needed answers to questions like "What the %$#&?!" O'Mahoney explained that in the mid-1950s, when he was in grade school, all he did was draw hot rod engines and rat rods. "We built Revel hot rod models of '32 roadsters and put Von Dutch pin stripe decals on our bikes," he said. "In the 1960s Big Daddy Roth did all kinds of drawings of monsters riding lawn mowers and skateboards—anything with wheels—and put huge, hopped-up engines in them. 'Surf Rat' is my combo 50s–60s concept come to reality. It's now on display in the museum and the response is unreal—a couple people said it was the best board there."

Board and photos courtesy Jim O'Mahoney and the Santa Barbara Surfing Museum

Buzzy's 1956 Scimitar

It was 1956 when Buzzy Trent laid out his big wave surfing design philosophy to Joe Quigg: "You don't hunt elephants with a BB gun or a pistol. You use an elephant gun." And it was 1956 when Quigg shaped this 11-foot balsa "Scimitar" for Buzzy Trent. The board is currently owned by John Mazza who, with the help of Les "The Birdman" Williams, was able to track down the history and ownership of the board, which was confirmed by Quigg. "The board apparently was well known at the time, and along with the Grey Ghost and a couple of other boards was actually known by its name. Scimitar was made by Quigg for Trent, but Trent returned it to Quigg who sold it to Tommy Zahn. Tommy Zahn's widow Dagmar was living with Malibu lifeguard Mike Young, so she gave Scimitar to him, and then he sold it to Allan Seymour who sold it to me. Quite a history of famous characters. The craftsmanship of the board is outstanding."

Shirley Wong's Big 10' 4" Curren Gun

According to Greg Lui-Kwan, this 10-foot, 4-inch balsa gun was made by Pat Curren, who shaped boards in the Kakaako district, in 1956 or 1957 for Shirley Wong, a member of the Chinese-Hawaiian Pung family. Greg says that many famous swimmers and watermen came from the Pung family, and they trained right

across the street from their waterfront home. Shirley Wong could no longer surf after being seriously injured in a car accident in the early 1960s. Lui-Kwan received the board from Wong's husband, Wallace Wong, in the late 1990s. The Curren balsa is in original mint condition with no restoration.

Photo by Greg Lui-Kwan

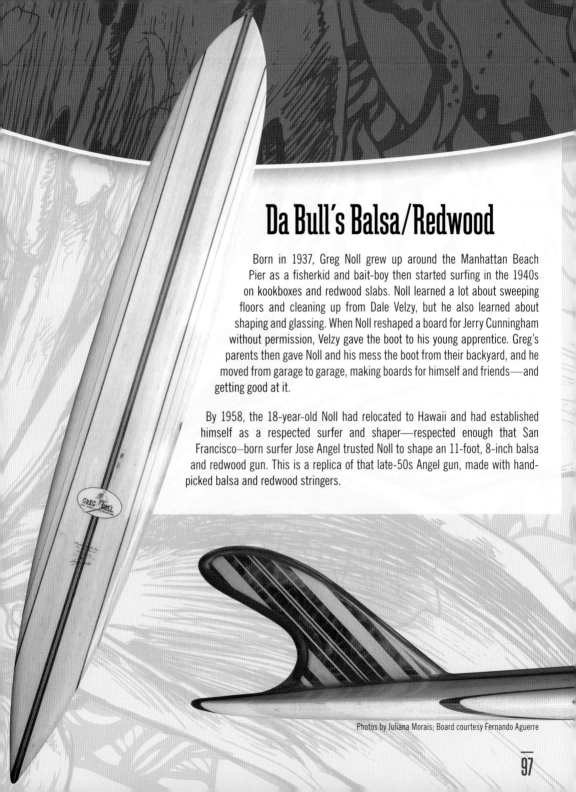

Da Bull's Balsa/Redwood

Born in 1937, Greg Noll grew up around the Manhattan Beach Pier as a fisherkid and bait-boy then started surfing in the 1940s on kookboxes and redwood slabs. Noll learned a lot about sweeping floors and cleaning up from Dale Velzy, but he also learned about shaping and glassing. When Noll reshaped a board for Jerry Cunningham without permission, Velzy gave the boot to his young apprentice. Greg's parents then gave Noll and his mess the boot from their backyard, and he moved from garage to garage, making boards for himself and friends—and getting good at it.

By 1958, the 18-year-old Noll had relocated to Hawaii and had established himself as a respected surfer and shaper—respected enough that San Francisco–born surfer Jose Angel trusted Noll to shape an 11-foot, 8-inch balsa and redwood gun. This is a replica of that late-50s Angel gun, made with hand-picked balsa and redwood stringers.

Photos by Juliana Morais; Board courtesy Fernando Aguerre

Greg Noll Gun

This meaty Greg Noll gun, from circa 1960, measures 12 feet long by 23 inches wide with a 16-inch nose and 12-inch tail; it's 4¼ inches thick. The double t-band stringer consists of five laminations: 3 inches of balsa and 1½ inches of redwood. According to current guardian Greg Lui-Kwan, the board "is serial numbered X-15 for the famous US spy plane launched on 11/15/60. The original owner Tai Sing Chow, a retired fireman, bought it in January of 1961 from the Greg Noll Shop on Waialae Avenue. When I got it from Mr. Chow in 1989, he told me Greg Noll called him asking to buy it back for the shooting of *Ride the Wild Surf*, which was filmed in 1963. Mr. Chow said no, he wanted to keep it. So I lucked out. This board features ahead-of-its-time super-hard down-rail edges in the rear and beveled rails in the front."

Joe Pang's Lightning Bolt

This gun features a Downing-inspired slotted hardwood fin box and was made by Joe Daniels of Swimm Boats fame for Joe Pang, a Waikiki beach boy and the father of Hawaiian shaper Dennis Pang. "Dad's favorite balsa board was that lightning bolt," Dennis Pang said. "However he did have a quiver of balsa boards. These were his favorite boards for about 10 years. When I started shaping in '69 and '70, he started getting boards from me. Many years later my mom said to get rid of the boards as they were taking up space at her house, so my brother and I sold them to Randy Rarick to put in his auction."

Collector Greg Lui-Kwan bought the board at a yard sale in the late 1990s. "I was bummed, figuring that some kid in the 1970s put some lightning bolt stickers on the board thinking that would be cute." But those lightning bolts are original art, according to Dennis Pang, who said his dad asked Daniels to put two lightning bolts in red paint on the nose. "Years later," Lui-Kwan said. "Dennis pointed out to Gerry Lopez . . . that Gerry wasn't the first one to put lightning bolts on surfboards—his dad was."

Photo by Greg Lui-Kwan

Bev Morgan's Pat Curren 12-Footer

Bev Morgan stands next to a 12-foot Pat Curren gun in about 1959 at Banzai Beach (soon to be known as Pipeline). Morgan detailed the genesis of this board in *Surfer Safari*, a story he wrote in April 1960. To make a long story short: In the late 1950s, Morgan flew to Hawaii and fell in love immediately. But he soon found his 9-foot, 6-inch mainland longboard wouldn't cut it in Hawaii. He drove over to Haleiwa, where he found Pat Curren and Al Nelson living like gentlemen in squalor in an abandoned railroad building. Morgan had cash. Curren was eating beans. They made a deal, and Curren got to it.

In his article, Morgan does not describe the construction of his surfboard, but he let the photographs tell the story, including a photo of Curren gluing up a balsa blank on the steps of the Moana Hotel at Waikiki. When the work was done, Morgan had a classic, 12-foot Curren gun. Morgan kept that board, and in 2013 he donated it to Dick Metz at the Surfing Heritage and Culture Center.

Photos courtesy John Elwell and Bev Morgan

Pat Curren Sunset Gun

Pat Curren started surfing relatively late—at the age of 18 in 1950—but by 1955 he had made the jump from La Jolla to Hawaii. He spent six thick years in Hawaii, challenging giant surf at Waimea and Sunset Beach and also establishing himself as one of the finest craftsmen of big-wave guns. His boards came out of trial and error—because to make an error in giant surf was a trial of getting pounded, half-drowning, and spending too much time swimming after your board. Simply, Curren wanted boards that would make the drop and make the wall at Waimea. By 1957 he was a regular at the Bay, and his boards were in very high demand. *The Surfer's Journal* referred to Curren's big-wave surfboards from the late 1950s as "the Ferrari of surf craft."

This Sunset gun was made in a time before surf leashes, when a mistake meant a long swim and possibly a lost surfboard. The leash loop seen at the base of the board was most likely added in the 1970s—a testament to the durability and relevance of a board made in 1959.

Board and photos courtesy John Mazza/Pepperdine University

Photos by Greg Lui-Kwan

Swimm Boat Balsa

In the late 1950s, shaper Bob Shepherd partnered with glasser Joe Daniels to open a surfboard-building operation with the odd name of Swimm Boats. Perhaps because of the name, Swimm Boats was a short-lived enterprise.

Shepherd was mentored by Joe Quigg, and this big-wave gun—a late-1950s-era 10-foot, 6-inch-long by 25-inch-wide balsa beauty—reflects that influence. Shepherd, in turn, is credited with mentoring Dick Brewer. According to Greg Lui-Kwan, "Dick Brewer once credited Bob Shepherd with teaching him everything he knew about shaping." Shepherd later shaped a few balsa guns for Brewer's Surfboards Hawaii, founded in 1960.

1961 Surfboards Hawaii Shepherd Balsa

This 10-foot, 6-inch by 22-inch by 3½-inch thick balsa gun was shaped by Bob Shepherd in 1961 for Surfboards Hawaii, a company founded by his student Dick Brewer. Born in California in 1934, Shepherd started surfing at 21, and two years later he was part of the coast *haole* migration to Hawaii. Shepherd learned to shape boards under the wing of Joe Quigg and soon found that he had the knack. His big-wave guns gained a following among surfers who needed boards that mattered—the likes of Paul Strauch and Buzzy Trent.

Photo by Greg Lui-Kwan

Inter-Island Sparky Elephant Gun

That's a big 10-foot, 4-inch Inter-Island elephant gun shaped by Robert "Sparky" Scheufele. As a shaper, Sparky is credited with developing concave nose designs and the first solid fiberglass surfboard fins, the first modern speed fin, the textured deck, and light glassing. He also named the surf spot known as Big Rights and initiated the environmental group Save Our Surf. Barry Morrison is the current owner of Inter-Island Surf Shop, and he had some back story: "Sparky was hired by Mickey Lake in 1961. Sparky had been selling his solid fiberglass fins to the shop. Mickey sold Sparky his Skill 100 planer and he was on his way. He used the planer until his final year and now it is with me." Sparky died on January 26, 2012, at the age of 77.

John Kelly 1964 Hydroplane

This 10-foot, 6-inch John Kelly Hydroplane is in the collection of Greg Lui-Kwan. The Surfing Heritage and Culture Center also has a Hydroplane in its collection, and their website quotes Kelly's 1965 book, *Surf and Sea*: "A favorite dream of surfers has always been to own a single all-time surfboard that combines the best of all existing designs, speed, maneuverability, stability; it should be a good paddler, easy to stall, slow to dig, yet good for nose-riding, stable and heavy-riding in rough water yet light to the touch in smooth."

Kelly explained in his book that he found the solution in a board that "consists of breaking the heretofore undifferentiated bottom surface into two surfaces, a longitudinally flat one for high-speed planing and a curved one for high-drag, low-

speed turning. The two surfaces are separated by means of a hydroplane step, the high-speed planing surface being located forward of the step and the curved one at the tail where the turning effect is located." Got it?

John Mazza's 10' 4" 1966 Hydroplane

John Mazza also has a beautiful, big 10-foot, 4-inch Hydroplane in his collection. This design is kind of hard to explain, but John Mazza said that Kelly sought to combine the speed of a longboard with the maneuverability of a shortboard. Ultimately, the design did not catch on with big-wave surfers, and the production of Hydroplane surfboards, such as this example by Inter-Island Surf Shop, quickly tapered off.

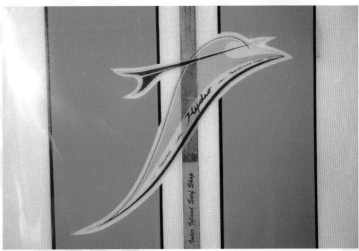

Board and photos courtesy John Mazza/Pepperdine University

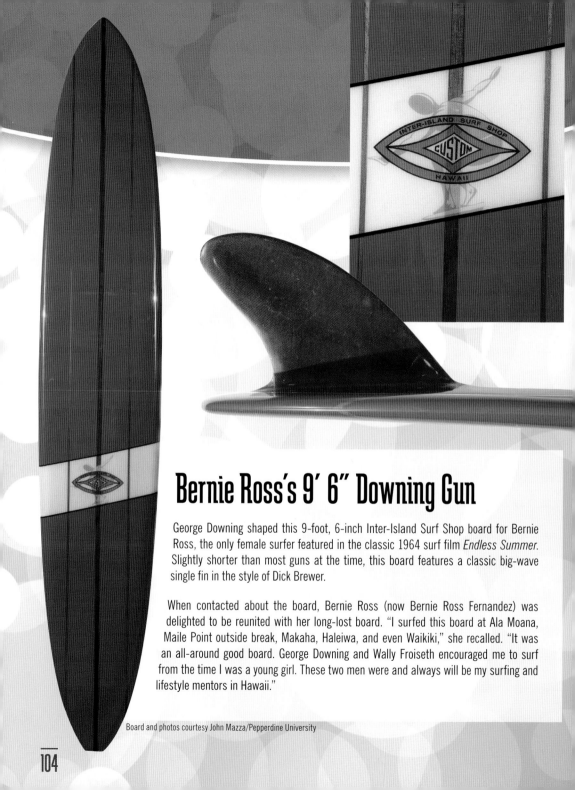

Bernie Ross's 9′ 6″ Downing Gun

George Downing shaped this 9-foot, 6-inch Inter-Island Surf Shop board for Bernie Ross, the only female surfer featured in the classic 1964 surf film *Endless Summer*. Slightly shorter than most guns at the time, this board features a classic big-wave single fin in the style of Dick Brewer.

When contacted about the board, Bernie Ross (now Bernie Ross Fernandez) was delighted to be reunited with her long-lost board. "I surfed this board at Ala Moana, Maile Point outside break, Makaha, Haleiwa, and even Waikiki," she recalled. "It was an all-around good board. George Downing and Wally Froiseth encouraged me to surf from the time I was a young girl. These two men were and always will be my surfing and lifestyle mentors in Hawaii."

Board and photos courtesy John Mazza/Pepperdine University

1965 Terry Martin 11' 2" Gun

Photo by Greg Lui-Kwan

This 11-foot, 2-inch Hobie gun dates back to 1965, and it was one of tens of thousands of boards shaped by Terry Martin. When Martin passed away of a melanoma in May 2012, memorials were held all over the surfing world. Martin spent most of his 60-year shaping career making boards for Hobie Alter, who first hired him in 1963. Before shaping machines were invented, Martin was a machine, plowing out as many as 10 boards a day, including signature models for Gary Propper, Corky Carroll, Gerry Lopez, Wayne "Rabbit" Bartholomew, and Joyce Hoffman. It's been estimated that he shaped as many as 80,000 boards in his life. Determining the exact number would require a forensic surfboardologist.

Noll and Aipa 9' 8" Gun

This 9-foot, 8-inch Greg Noll gun was shaped by Ben Aipa in late 1967 when pintails were popular. It has a ¾-inch redwood stringer, a yellow opaque bottom with black pins, a yellow tint deck with black pin, and double Greg Noll laminates. The board was up for sale at the 2001 Hawaiian Islands Vintage Surf Auction, where it sold for $2,000.

Photos by Juliana Morais; Board courtesy Fernando Aguerre

Hobie-Brewer #83

The Dick Brewer timeline is layered with eras and epochs, and just about all the layers had a profound effect on the evolution of the surfboard. The Hobie-Brewer epoch arrived in 1965 when Brewer left Surfboards Hawaii to go work for Hobie Alter.

According to Drew Kampion, Brewer shaped 88 guns for Hobie, working from a small shop in Wahiawa, between Waikiki and the North Shore. Brewer shaped, glassed, sanded, and glossed every one of these boards, and they made a name for themselves pretty fast; Jeff Hakman won the Duke Kahanamoku Invitational on a Hobie-Brewer gun during the winter of 1965–1966. These Hobie-Brewer guns are now collectors' items in the surfboard aficionado world.

Greg Lui-Kwan has in his collection 3 of the 88 Hobie-Brewer boards that were produced. The one shown here is #83; he also is the proud owner of #44 and #52. He loves them all equally.

Photos by Greg Lui-Kwan

Roberts and Hobie Custom Longboards

Stuart Matthews, seen in the photo standing with his friend Tom Cundall, is the owner of two near-pristine blasts from the past. Matthews acquired the boards in December 2012 from a guy in Gloucestershire in rural England where the boards had been stored in a barn for more than 40 years. Cundall's uncle, Bob Dunlop, had commissioned Bob Millner from Roberts Surfboards in Playa Del Rey to make the 9-foot, 9-inch blue longboard. Dunlop rode it a few times in 1959 in California, and Cornwall then gave it to his family. He then traveled to Hawaii where he met Hobie Alter, who shaped the 10-foot, 6-inch brown board. According to Matthews, Hobie president Mark Christy is the owner of one of the largest private Hobie collections, and he believes this brown board is among the most pristine unrestored boards he has come across. The Roberts custom is a similarly rare find.

Courtesy Stuart Matthews

1958 Greg Noll
Foam Longboard with Huge Fin

This 9-foot, 2-inch Greg Noll longboard is wide in the hips and might be a riff on Dale Velzy's Pig. The "Greg Noll — Surf Boards and Film Productions" cameraman logo dates this board anywhere from 1955 to 1958, which is on the cusp of the balsa to foam transition.

Photos by Juliana Morais-Board courtesy Fernando Aguerre

Photo © John Severson

Greg Noll loved working with wood in the 1950s and still does to this day, but regardless of his love for mowing balsa, as the decade moved along, Noll saw the scribbling on the walls of shaping rooms all over southern California, and he got gritty. Noll reflected on the pros and cons of foam in his book *Greg Noll: The Art of the Surfboard*: "It was absolutely terrible! It was soulless. With balsa—if you have the right tools and can get a bitchin' piece of wood—every piece of wood is different. It has a nice, mellow feel, a nice look. . . . But as far as a medium for surfboards, foam had its advantages; its weight was consistent, it was much easier to shape, and there was less waste. But the big thing was, with foam, you were able to flow with the design evolution much easier than with balsa."

The Morrissey Brothers' Noll and Hobie Longboards

"The Longboard Brothers"—Keith Kyle, Mike, and Steve Morrissey—have a barn filled with classic longboards and surf memorabilia, including a light blue Greg Noll board from the early 1960s. It still features the rare Fatman logo and the "Greg Noll" logo in red print. The blue Hobie, which Keith acquired for a mere $200, is a well-made board featuring an early keel fin, most likely from the late 1950s or early '60s. It is a triple stringer with ¾-inch balsa encased in ¼-inch redwood and is completely original and unrestored except to make it water tight and rideable. Steve explained how this board made it into the barn: "I bought it on College Hill in Providence, Rhode Island. Bitter cold with 8 inches of fresh powder. Had $150 in one pocket and another $150 in the other. The seller wanted $300. It was so cold I emptied both pockets and ran down Benefit Street past the courthouse in a suit and tie in a blizzard—Hobie under arm!"

Photo by Joe McGovern

1960 John Severson's
Surf Fever Art Board

In 2005 the Surfrider Foundation presented Art for the Oceans, a surfboard-art auction to raise money to support the foundation's quest to protect oceans, waves, and beaches. Thirty-six Fish boards made by Al Merrick served as canvases for surfing artists and artists who surf. John Severson is a lifetime surfer and artist, and he painted this board with images from his 1960 movie *Surf Fever*. "It seemed that the 1960 *Surf Fever* image fit the fish," Severson said. "So I jumped the image 45 years into the future to help save the oceans. The board is a mixed media piece. I digitalized the graphics from the original poster and printed them on rice paper. The rice paper images were glued on to the board and then defined with acrylics."

Courtesy Surfrider Foundation

Joe Quigg 10′ 10″ Paddleboard

This 10-foot, 10-inch foam paddleboard dates from around 1960 and was made by Joe Quigg, whose enthusiasm for plastics raised eyebrows in and out of the surfing world. As Nat Young described it in *The History of Surfing*, "Because of his diligent enquiries to every chemical company in Los Angeles, Joe Quigg was suspected of being a German spy!" This board was one of about 20 paddleboards Quigg made in the early 1960s, all of them under 11 feet and all with a fin. This one has a balsa stringer, Foss foam, and was glassed with Volan cloth. The board was restored by Randy Rarick.

Photo by Juliana Morais; Board courtesy Fernando Aguerre

Gordie Longboard

This longboard was made by Gordon "Gordie" Duane, who was also known as the "Compton Cabinet Maker." After moving to Huntington Beach in 1956, Duane inherited a surfboard shop from Rocky Freeman—a garage on the sand at the base of the Huntington Pier that had the "Gordie Man" mounted over the garage door entry. His heyday was the 1950s into the 1960s, when Huntington Beach was Surf City and the center of the surfing world. When his garage shop burned, Gordie moved to the inland side of the Pacific Coast Highway, a mile or so north from the pier. From this bastion, the 1960s and '70s rolled by, during which Gordie's "Hole in the Fence" crew of hot local riders with rebel inclinations was formed. It was during this later period that the Gordie shield board was produced, probably for a team rider like Bubby Hill, Robert Kooken, John Boozer, Randy Lewis, or Frog Van Offlen. "Gordie was more greaser than water guy," Steve Pezman said. "And the combo gave him a uniqueness that separated him from the more esthetic builders."

Photo by Joe McGovern

Joe Quigg's Prop Board for *Blue Hawaii*

There was a rumor around Malibu that someone down in Latigo had a Joe Quigg board that was used in Elvis Presley's *Blue Hawaii*. That rumor led to the garage of Mr. Armstrong, a long-time Latigo resident. Hiding behind some antique cars, this beat-up board was more sun-damaged than some of the women who live in Malibu. The collector's son Alan said that his father bought the board from Mickey Moore, who lived down the street and was an assistant director on *Blue Hawaii*. "He got that board from *Blue Hawaii*, and my dad bought it from him," Alan continued. "It was a kick-around board. We rode it right out here in the surf."

Photos by Ben Marcus; Board courtesy the Armstrong family

1962–1964 Shark Popout

This Shark surfboard was made by both man and machine, as it's what 1960s surfers called a "popout"—meaning the board was molded in a machine and not shaped by the hand of man. According to Stoked 'n Board, the Shark logo was one of many brands produced by Pacific Plastics, which was a division of Ventura International Plastics and operated on Olive Street in Ventura by Jack Herron from 1957 to 1965 and by Bill Fisher and Sam Gillard from 1965 to 1968. Tom Hale did hand-shape some custom boards, but Pacific Plastics mostly produced popouts under the brands Duke Kahanamoku, Inland Surfer, Sting Ray, Ten Toes, Tiki, Ventura Surfboards, Westwind, and Shark. The latter were produced from 1962 to 1964, 9-foot boards with matt glass and a glassed-on single fin. Which is what we seem to have here.

Photos by Juliana Morais; Board courtesy Fernando Aguerre

Photos by Lucia Griggi; Board courtesy John Mazza

1962 Quigg Foam Board with Huge Stringer

Joe Quigg was still going strong making surfboards in 1962, firmly in the foam and fiberglass evolution. But apparently he still had a thing for balsa, as the stringer in this 9-foot by 22-inch by 3⅛-inch board looks to be about 4 inches thick. According the board's owner, John Mazza, the board has two 1-inch balsa stringers laminated together. "Quigg shut down the Newport Beach factory about 1962," Mazza explained, "and that is when he really stopped making all balsa boards."

John Moore's Gordie with a Cool Fin

Fashion designer, high-end surf brander, and "vintage freak" John Moore is the proud owner of this 1962 Gordie, bought from the Vintage Board Swap near the Venice Pier. "Paid a few hundred bucks at the bottom of the recession," Moore recalled. "Someone just recently told me that Gordie was the first shaper to put his logo laminates under the glass of surfboards." He hasn't measured the board to get its dimensions, but it's the longest in his collection—about 10 feet—and heavy. "For me, this board has always been about the fin. It's a wood fin with what appears to be more than 60 pieces of wood, three different species, puzzle pieced together for one of the most beautifully assembled fins I have ever seen."

Photos courtesy John Moore

Early 1960s Harry Stanbury Longboard

This Harry Stanbury board, being shown off by owner Alex Williams, was made between 1962 and 1964 and was at the forefront of British boards. According to Williams, "The blank was refrigerator foam which was blown in Stanbury's front room and glassed in Roger Harry's house! It has been covered in blue gloss paint for many years and is in the process of being uncovered."

Courtesy Alex Williams

1963 Hobie Phil Edwards Signature Model

Despite his quote, "Spastic on plastic, good on wood," Phil Edwards finally jumped into plastics in the early 1960s, and he jumped in name-first. This 10-foot Phil Edwards signature model was the first signature board of any kind. It was produced and sold by Hobie Surfboards beginning in 1963. Compare this board to the replica of Edwards's 1958 "Baby" balsa that Wingnut Weaver proudly displayed earlier in this book, and you'll note a similar shape, which Edwards carried over into foam and fiberglass.

Two years after producing this signature model, Edwards and Hobie would team up to design a fleet of noseriders that the Hobie team would use to dominate the first professional surfing contest: the Tom Morey Invitational held at C Street in Ventura on July 4, 1965.

Board and photos courtesy John Mazza/Pepperdine University

Bird's Olympic Longboard

Olympic Surfboards was founded by Bill Caster in late 1959, when he was just 17 years old. Olympic's main shapers at the time were Bill Caster and Mike Diffenderfer, one of whom likely shaped this green board in about 1962. It was around this time that Caster left to start Caster Surfboards, leaving Olympic to investor Phil Castagnola, who later sold it to the Bahne Brothers. Like so many other brands, Olympic never made the transition to shortboards, however, and eventually stopped production altogether. Phil Castagnola Jr. tried to jump-start the name again in the 1990s with no real success.

According to Eric "Bird" Huffman of Bird's Surf Shed, the board was a raffle prize at a local surf movie. "To this day the board has never seen the water and, with the exceptions of some small knocks and scratches, is in pristine condition."

Photo by Chris Park; Board courtesy Bird's Surf Shed

Bruce Brown's
Final Phil Edwards Balsa

Up a quiet canyon along the Gaviota Coast, Bruce Brown lives in a ranch house surrounded by mementos and memories from a long, accomplished, fun-filled life. A submariner and surf movie mogul in the 1950s, Brown is best-known for producing and directing the motorcycle documentary *On Any Sunday* and the surfing doc *Endless Summer* in the 1960s.

Arguably the coolest thing on any of the walls is the photo of Bruce Brown hanging with Steve McQueen on a float plane in Alaska circa the 1960s. You could argue that the Phil Edwards three-stringer balsa Bruce stood with is pretty cool, too. Edwards gave the board to Brown as a gift. "It was the foam board era and good balsa was hard to get," Brown recalled. "Phil told me 'that is the last balsa board I'm going to make.' And it was, except for the more recent 'wall hangers.' I took it out once at Doheny and it got center-punched by a foam board with the nose broken off and the stringer sticking out. Put a nasty hole in it that recently got fixed by Wingnut."

Photos by Lucia Griggi/Lensbaby

1964 G&S Balsa for Ernie Tanaka

By 1964, balsa was about as passé as 8-track tapes are today, but this 10-foot, 5-inch by 22-inch balsa board was made by the San Diego–based Gordon & Smith for team rider Ernie Tanaka. According to Paul Holmes and Chris Dixon of the Honolulu Surfing Museum, this board was shaped by Dana Duke at the special request of team rider Ernie Tanaka and was possibly the last balsa board produced by G&S. Tanaka earned an engineering degree from UCLA and launched Ernie Tanaka Surfboards in Van Nuys, California. He returned to Hawaii in the late 1970s where he shaped for Town & Country, Blue Hawaii Surf, and Local Motion. Tanaka died of a heart attack in 1998, but his son Tommy carries on the family tradition as a surfboard maker in Honolulu.

Board and photos courtesy Jimmy Buffett/Honolulu Surfing Museum

10' 2" Hobie
Shaped by Hynson

This beautiful, 10-foot, 2-inch Hobie was shaped by Mike Hynson for Butch van Artsdalen, who has one of the coolest names in surf history. Van Artsdalen was a product of the hard-drinking, hard-surfing, hard-partying Windansea Surf Club crew. During the winter of 1962 van Artsdalen found his feet on the North Shore of Oahu and pushed many limits, including switching foot at big Waimea Bay and riding deeper in the tube at Pipeline than anyone had before dared. Butch rode this board at Pipeline and Sunset.

MVP Books collection

Photos by Juliana Morais; Board courtesy Fernando Aguerre

1964 9′ 3″ Yater Spoon

In the famous "Charlie don't surf!" scene from the movie *Apocalypse Now*, when Colonel William "Bill" Kilgore was bellowing for someone to fetch his Yater Spoon, this was the kind of board he was bellowing about. Colonel Kilgore wanted his "eight-six," but this is a 9-foot, 3-inch board, made in 1964 by Reynolds Yater.

Yater glassed for Hobie in Dana Point and shaped balsa boards for Dale Velzy before opening Yater Surfboards in Santa Barbara in 1959. Here he established the famous Santa Barbara Surf Shop logo. In the mid-1960s, he shaped the Yater Spoon. Made for California point surf like Rincon, the Yater Spoon had a wide, round, upturned nose that prevented the board from pearling—the foam and fiberglass riff on Bob Simmons's "scarfed" noses of a decade before.

Board and photos courtesy John Mazza/Pepperdine University

John Mazza's 9' 6" Wardy

John Mazza grew up in San Clemente in the late 1950s and then lived off and on in Laguna until he moved to Malibu in 1972. This flawless 9-foot, 6-inch by 23-inch Wardy reminds him of those days in the OC, when he loved surfing Trestles. "Everyone who grew up in south Orange County in the '60s knew Wardy surfboards," recalled Mazza. "After Hobie left Laguna Beach to move to Dana Point, Wardy was the shop of choice in Laguna Beach. Fred Wardy was a fine artist, a sculptor, a great craftsman, and ad writer. In the late '60s (I think) he closed up shop and moved to the East Coast to chase his dream of becoming an artist. He joined the artist/surfer ranks of John Severson, John Van Hammersveld, Billy Al Bengston, Ken Price, and Craig Stecyk, among others."

Photos by Lucia Griggi; Board courtesy John Mazza

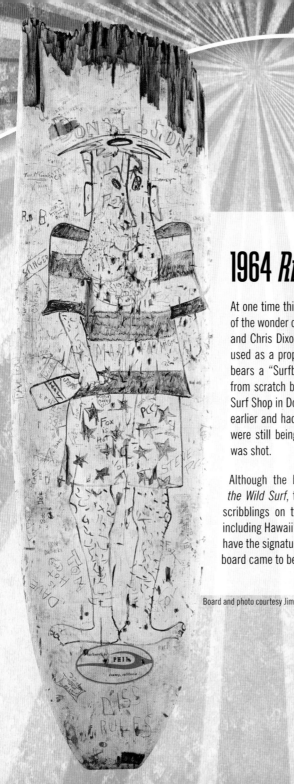

1964 *Ride the Wild Surf* Balsa

At one time this 6-foot, 11-inch balsa was new and fresh and full of the wonder of life. So what happened? According to Paul Holmes and Chris Dixon of the Honolulu Surfing Museum, this board was used as a prop in the 1964 movie *Ride the Wild Surf*. The board bears a "Surfboards by Phil" logo, but it's unlikely it was made from scratch by the trademark's owner, Phil Sauers of the Inland Surf Shop in Downey, California. It was probably made some years earlier and had the logo added to it, since very few balsa boards were still being produced in the winter of 1963 when the movie was shot.

Although the board was clean when it was featured in *Ride the Wild Surf*, there are now all kinds of notes, autographs, and scribblings on the board. All manner of surfers have signed it, including Hawaii's legendary Rabbit Kekai, but it does not appear to have the signatures of the film's principal stars. It's unclear how the board came to be broken.

Board and photo courtesy Jimmy Buffett/Honolulu Surfing Museum

Photo by Tatsuo Takei

Kio Inagaki's Replica Phil Edwards Baby Balsa

Kio Inagaki, founder of Yellow Rat, stands with a 9-foot, 10¾-inch by 22-inch Phil Edwards Baby Balsa replica, shaped for him by the late Mike Marshall. According to Kio, it is a replica of the board Edwards rode in the Bruce Brown film *Surfing Hollow Days*, which was shaped by Joe Quigg. Marshall told Kio that the board's 9-foot, 10¾-inch length was the "magic number." It was the last board that Marshall shaped for Kio.

The board sits in the middle of the transition of two other Marshall-shaped replica boards in Kio's collection: a late-1950s model Malibu Chip and a 1960s-era Trestle Special. The Malibu Chip, made of foam and fiberglass and shaped in 2003, was the first lightweight board Marshall shaped for him. The Trestle Special was the first board Marshall ever shaped for Kio, in 1986. It was based on Marshall's best-selling boards when he worked at Harbour Surfboards in the 1960s, and the original template came from Joe Quigg. Marshall once told Kio that Quigg's boards were "between art piece and machine."

Photo by Lucia Griggi; Boards courtesy Kio Inagaki

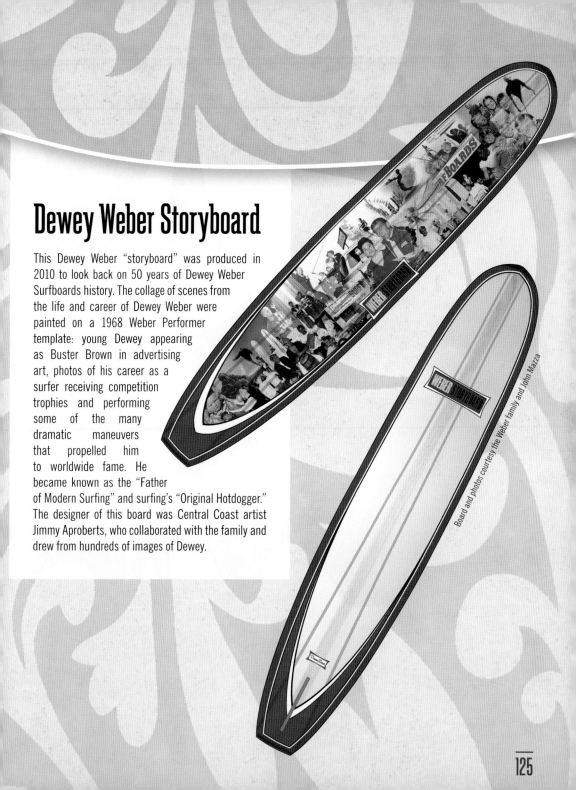

Dewey Weber Storyboard

This Dewey Weber "storyboard" was produced in 2010 to look back on 50 years of Dewey Weber Surfboards history. The collage of scenes from the life and career of Dewey Weber were painted on a 1968 Weber Performer template: young Dewey appearing as Buster Brown in advertising art, photos of his career as a surfer receiving competition trophies and performing some of the many dramatic maneuvers that propelled him to worldwide fame. He became known as the "Father of Modern Surfing" and surfing's "Original Hotdogger." The designer of this board was Central Coast artist Jimmy Aproberts, who collaborated with the family and drew from hundreds of images of Dewey.

Board and photos courtesy the Weber family and John Mazza

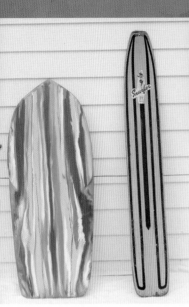

1950 Paipo Board and 1965 Snurfer

The green, lozengy-looking board on the left is, in the words of John Mazza, a "super rare Bob Simmons Slot Paipo. John Elwell said Simmons made very few since he only made them when he %*@#ed-up a Slot-board blank when he was shaping them, and he made very few Slots in the early 1950s."

Photo by Lucia Griggi; Boards courtesy John Mazza

The board to the right is a Snurfer, a cross between a surfer and a snow ski that would eventually beget the snowboard. The Snurfer was first developed in 1965 by Sherman Poppen of Muskegon, Michigan. He was inspired by his 11-year-old daughter sliding down a snowy hill, standing on her sled. Poppen bound together two skis and connected a piece of string to the nose that the rider could use for control. Poppen's wife dubbed it the "Snurfer." Poppen licensed the concept to Brunswick Corporation to manufacture the Snurfer—and they sold a million of them from 1966 to 1976.

1965–1967 Reef 9′ 2″ Popout

This Reef surfboard is part of the vast collection of surfboards owned by the guy who started Reef Brazil Sandals—but do you think he knows it's a popout? It is, according to the Stoked 'n Board website, which declares that Reef was one of four brands produced from 1965 to 1967 by Surfcraft of Jacksonville, Florida. Owner Allen Faas produced the Mako, Marin, Surfcraft, and Reef models, and they were sold from the Surfcraft factory or East Coast K-Mart Stores. This 9-foot, 2-inch Reef longboard had a balsa/redwood t-band, a laminated wood nose, and tail. The model came in 9-foot, 2-inch; 9-foot, 4-inch; 9-foot, 6-inch; 9-foot, 8-inch, or 10-foot sizes. The boards were glassed with two layers of 10.6-ounce glass on the deck and bottom and had double-wrapped rails, which all added up to a 40-pound package.

Marc Andreini's White Owl Replicas

Marc Andreini owns several replica White Owl surfboards based on the boards that were ridden around southern California in the 1960s. Andreini, who now lives in San Mateo County where he crafts beautiful surfboards out of both wood and plastic, has been obsessed with surfboards since he was 12 years old when he was growing up in Santa Barbara and was best friends with Margo Godfrey. Andreini remembers sneaking Margo and some friends into the Hollister Ranch north of Santa Barbara and seeing George Greenough paddle his Velo kneeboard out into perfect waves at Government Point. "When you witness the surfing of Greenough," Andreini was quoted in *Liquid Salt Magazine*, "there are just no words to describe what you've just seen,

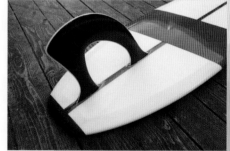

Photos by Paul Ferraris; Boards courtesy Marc Andreini

and I was fortunate to be a witness of it. Like the Australians, I wanted to figure out how I could surf like Greenough but standing up." Andreini took his brother's White Owl surfboard and cut it down to a 7-foot, 2-inch arc tail stubbie—and that began another 50-plus years of innovation in surfboard shaping.

1965 Morey-Pope Trisect

Air travel was glamorous in the 1960s. Pilots were rock stars, flight attendants were knockouts, and travelers would dress up in their Sunday best. But traveling with a 10-foot-plus, heavy longboard was almost as much of an expensive pain then as it is now. So Karl Pope and Tom Morey came up with a surfboard that could be separated into three pieces for easy transportation. Pope and Morey made a promotional film in the mid-1960s, in which they explained the origins of the Trisect. "It all started back in 1964, when we built the first Trisect," Pope said. "Tom Morey and I took a Mexicana flight to Mazatlan and then on to San Blas for the first test of the Trisect in actual surfing conditions. The first Trisects were heavy, like 40 pounds. They were double-glassed with 10-ounce cloth, and lots of clamps at each junction."

Photos by Lucia Griggi; Board courtesy John Mazza

1965 Renny Yater Longboard for Bob Cooper

An inscription on the foam, just below the Santa Barbara Surf Shop label, tells part of the story on this board: "One for the Coop's — enjoy old friend. Renny Yater." According to the board's current owner, John Mazza, Yater made the board for Bob Cooper to keep in Santa Barbara and use when he visited from Australia, where Coop expatriated himself in 1969. Cooper was a major figure in California surfing through the 1960s.

Photos by Lucia Griggi; Board courtesy John Mazza

Jed Noll's Red Bull Replicas of Da Bull's Pipeline Board

Son of Da Bull, Jed Noll has a cool surf shop and a thriving business in San Clemente, where he produces classic boards in hardwoods and modern boards in foam and fiberglass. These yellow guns are replicas of the board that his father famously used to paddle into a giant, outer reef bomb at Third Reef Pipeline in 1964 (see page 108). "Red Bull ordered five of them, but details are a little muddy on what they intend to do with them," Jed said. "I guess they are going to have five of their team riders ride five boards from different generations."

Photo by Ben Marcus; Board courtesy Jed Noll Surfboards

Photo by Lucia Griggi; Boards courtesy Jed Noll Surfboards

The yellow boards are 11 feet, 3 inches. Jed did the best he could to keep the replicas true to the original. "Weight is going to be a little less, but I did glass them with Volan," the younger Noll said. "We didn't use double 10-ounce cloth like in my dad's day. But we used two cloth layers of Volan 7.5 and double hot-coated them and double-glossed them. The boards have a ¾-inch stringer. US Blanks glues up our rocker and stringer thickness. I built these all together in January 2013, which is a good month for a project like this."

1965 Duke Kahanamoku Popout

This beautifully crafted, multi-stringered 9-foot, 6-inch longboard was made in the name of Duke Kahanamoku—Olympic hero and Johnny Appleseed of surfing. Who shaped this beauty? What? It's a *popout*?! Apparently so, according to the Stoked 'n Board website, which says Duke Kahanamoku owned a company that produced surfboards from a factory in Honolulu from 1965 to 1968 and in El Segundo, California, from 1968 to 2012. The boards were made from popout blanks by Ventura International Plastics and the models were the Butch van Artsdalen Custom, the Classic 9 feet, 6 inches to 10 feet, 2 inches; the Hawaii Sport(flite) 9 feet, 8 inches; the Maui, the Nose Rider, and the Performer 8 feet, 6 inches to 9 feet, 1 inch. This board is 9 feet, 6 inches and is most likely The Classic.

Felipe Pomar's 10' 4" Greg Noll World Beater

Courtesy Felipe Pomar

Felipe Pomar is shown posing with the 10-foot, 4-inch Greg Noll semi-gun that he rode to victory at the 1965 World Contest, held at Punta Rocas, just outside of Lima. "That board was built to take to Peru and compete in the 1965 World Championships," Pomar said. "The shaper was Rick James. Obviously it was a good board." Indeed. Felipe rode it to become the first Latin American surfing champion in a final that included Nat Young and Fred Hemmings, both of whom earned world titles in the 1960s. After the competition, Pomar gave the board to Carlos Dogny, who helped introduce modern surfing to Peru and founded Club Waikiki.

1966 Bilbo 9' 6" with Mystery Numbers

Alex Williams sent this 9-foot, 6-inch 1966 Bilbo and explained that it was shaped for somebody named Mr. Backmann. According to Williams, the numbers printed at the top of the board have to do with its registration for insurance. The board is 9 feet, 6¾ inches long by 22¾ inches wide by 3⅝ inches thick and has an early example of nylon-cast fins. "It has the typical Bilbo Swirl," said Williams, "until you put the board on its side and it is a perfect peak!"

Asked for more details on the board registration, which is something Newport Beach did in California in the 1960s, Tony Cope couldn't recall that ever being done in England but suspects it is the registration number for an Aussie board hire company. "Big numbers like that generally mean: 'Don't steal this board, because it's too easy to spot it's one of ours!'"

Photo by Alex Williams

Mazza's 9' 11" Phil Edwards Honolulu Model

In 1966, Phil Edwards moved to Hawaii and, for a two-year period, made a small number of surfboards under the label "Phil Edwards Honolulu." John Mazza has a beautiful brown and white Edwards Honolulu board in his collection. It is 9 feet, 11 inches by 22 inches and is numbered A 15. According to Mazza, Edwards very quickly changed his boards as shortboards started becoming more popular. The A and B models were pretty close to each other in size, but by the C model they got substantially shorter. He progressed to D and E models before he closed up shop.

Photos by Lucia Griggi; Board courtesy John Mazza

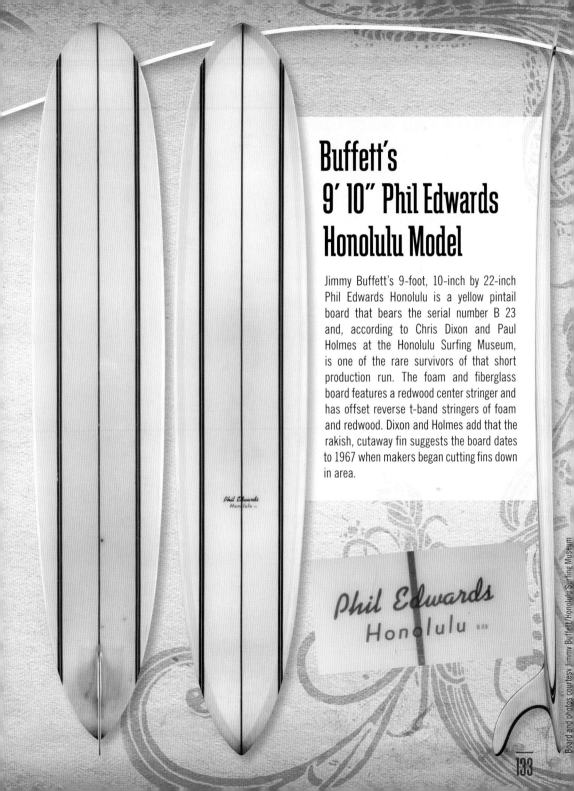

Buffett's 9' 10" Phil Edwards Honolulu Model

Jimmy Buffett's 9-foot, 10-inch by 22-inch Phil Edwards Honolulu is a yellow pintail board that bears the serial number B 23 and, according to Chris Dixon and Paul Holmes at the Honolulu Surfing Museum, is one of the rare survivors of that short production run. The foam and fiberglass board features a redwood center stringer and has offset reverse t-band stringers of foam and redwood. Dixon and Holmes add that the rakish, cutaway fin suggests the board dates to 1967 when makers began cutting fins down in area.

Phil Edwards Honolulu

Board and photos courtesy Jimmy Buffett/Honolulu Surfing Museum

Board and photos courtesy Jimmy Buffett and the Honolulu Surfing Museum

1967 Noll–Dora Da Cat Original

This original 10-foot by 23-inch black Da Cat was made in 1967 of foam and fiberglass and is currently in the collection of the Honolulu Surfing Museum, courtesy of Jimmy Buffett. The 1960s produced a menagerie of branded surfboard models: Performer, Pipeliner, Ugly, Bug, Tiger Stripe, Eliminator, and dozens of others. Of all those models, few have as interesting a history and epilogue as Da Cat. The product of a tenuous partnership between twitchy rebel Miki Dora and all-business Greg Noll, Da Cat was made for California point surfing, and it first became available in 1966. The board's selling point was the distinctively sculpted deck, plus it was specifically designed to be shorter, wider, and lighter than other surfboards of the day. Dimensions of a typical Da Cat were a 17-inch nose, a wide point of 22½ inches, and a squared-off tail area of 16 inches.

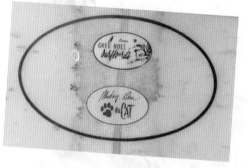

The board was good, but the ad campaign was a classic, devised by Dora and Noll with nudging from Duke Boyd. Da Cat rode the crest of Dora's notoriety as a rebel who flipped off the commercialization of surfing with one hand and picked its pocket with the other.

Author's collection

1992 Noll–Dora Da Cat Replica

Da Cat rose again in 1992, when Laura Noll brokered a deal between Greg Noll and Miki Dora to make replicas of Da Cat. The first 250 boards—featuring artwork depicting Miki Dora as some kind of World War I German fighter ace—were made of foam and fiberglass and began selling for $1,000; they soon went up to $5,000. There was an additional run of 50 hardwood Da Cats. In 1995, a guy named Rick Pharaoh was arrested for making copycat Da Cats out of his garage in Canoga Park.

Photos by Juliana Morais; Board courtesy Fernando Aguerre

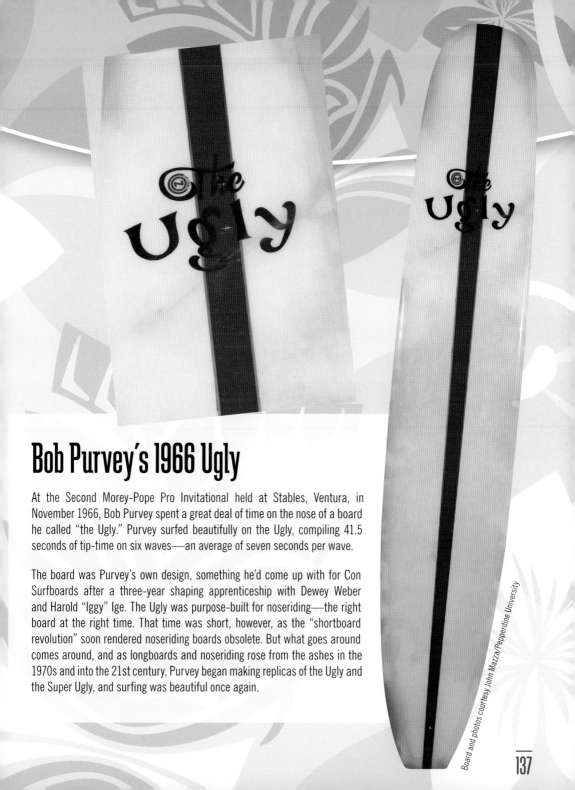

Bob Purvey's 1966 Ugly

At the Second Morey-Pope Pro Invitational held at Stables, Ventura, in November 1966, Bob Purvey spent a great deal of time on the nose of a board he called "the Ugly." Purvey surfed beautifully on the Ugly, compiling 41.5 seconds of tip-time on six waves—an average of seven seconds per wave.

The board was Purvey's own design, something he'd come up with for Con Surfboards after a three-year shaping apprenticeship with Dewey Weber and Harold "Iggy" Ige. The Ugly was purpose-built for noseriding—the right board at the right time. That time was short, however, as the "shortboard revolution" soon rendered noseriding boards obsolete. But what goes around comes around, and as longboards and noseriding rose from the ashes in the 1970s and into the 21st century, Purvey began making replicas of the Ugly and the Super Ugly, and surfing was beautiful once again.

Board and photos courtesy John Mazza/Pepperdine University

1966–1968 Weber Performer

This original Dewey Weber Performer represents what Shea Weber, son of shaper Dewey Weber, once proclaimed the "most popular single surfboard model in history." Weber's Performer was the first surfboard given a model name. The younger Weber also explained (to Tom Fucigna Jr. for an article in the Cocoa Beach Surf Museum's *Wavelength* publication), "People think the Performer was designed as a noserider, but that's not true! It's a great noserider, but my dad was a hotdogger, a high performance turn style surfer. There is no way that he would have designed a surfboard that didn't turn on a dime."

Photos by Juliana Morais; Board courtesy Fernando Aguerre

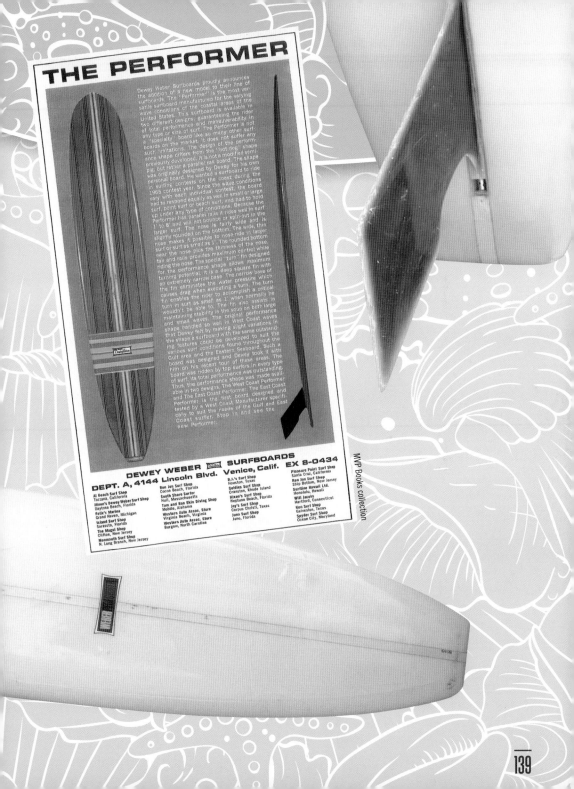

MVP Books collection

1967 Chuck Dent Experience

Chuck Dent started surfing in 1959 at the age of 16, and he worked for Jack Haley Surfboards in Seal Beach before opening his own shop in Huntington Beach. He was kind of the Orange County version of Miki Dora—ranting in the movies *Pacific Vibrations* and *Five Summer Stories* about the commercialization of surfing while selling boards with a team that included Barry Kanaiapuni and Mark Martinson.

Texas surfboard collector Mark Troutman now owns this board, and he explained that this 7-foot, 2-inch board was one of the rare Chuck Dent "Obscene" laminate label boards—most bore the "Jimi Hendrix Experience" mural, which is where the name Experience came from. Troutman noted that the image of the naked girl caused quite a stir when the board was released.

Troutman acquired the board from a former team rider for Dent from the early 1970s. "This was one of his [Dent's] favorite riders," said Troutman, "and had traveled with him throughout South America as well as all the U.S. breaks." The rider bought the board new at Lloyd's Surf House in Houston, where Dent would come and shape for a few months each year in the late 1960s and early '70s.

Photos by Jim and Mark Troutman, courtesy www.thesurfboardproject.com

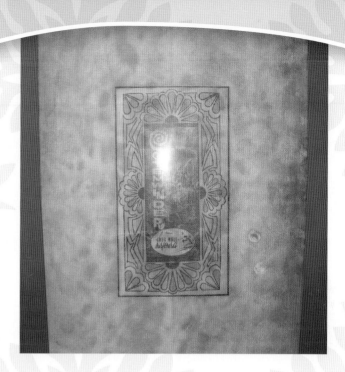

Greg Noll Stemwinder

Greg Noll is one of the pioneers of the surf-industrial complex, and he was clever when it came to branding surfboards in the 1960s: The Bug, Da Cat, and this, the Stemwinder. The board was made in a very limited run for maybe a month in 1967, and most of the boards were shipped to the East Coast.

According to Greg Noll in his book *Greg Noll: The Art of the Surfboard*, "Generally speaking, there was a reason for every surfboard that you did, and there's a story behind every board . . . even the Stemwinders." Noll said the Stemwinder was designed and produced during a time when LSD and other hallucinogens were popular. Guys would work on them all night long, and the LSD influence can be seen in the label. "A horrific description of Dante's Inferno," Noll said, "with all these guys sticking forks in each other's asses and guys with horns—just the perfect deal, like something you'd see on a bum trip on LSD or something."

Greg Noll Eight-Footer

The shortboard revolution changed the surfboard market almost overnight. Surfboard makers who had warehouses full of traditional 10-footers began to panic as they saw their very expensive inventory become obsolete. According to Matt Warshaw's *History of Surfing*, panicky manufacturers threatened an advertising boycott, which inspired John Severson at *Surfer* magazine to lean off shortboard coverage until September 1968, after shops were able to pass off their dying inventory during the summer months. A lot of good, bad, and ugly boards were shaped and shipped from 1966 well into the 1970s. This 8-foot board is a fairly clean transitional shape, most likely chopped down from a longer board; Greg Noll had been down that road before, as in the 1950s he learned to shape by taking down Pacific Systems Homes planks into boards that were lighter, faster, and more modern.

Photo by Juliana Morais; Board courtesy Fernando Aguerre

1967 Bilbo 10-Footer

Stuart Matthews is an English tidal bore rider extraordinaire. Way before it was cool to do so, Matthews led a crew of English types to have a go at surfing the powerful Silver Dragon tidal bore that roars up the Qiantang River in southeastern China. Before he was traveling the world to surf, however, Matthews got his start in the mid-1960s off the Channel Island of Jersey. He had always ridden imported Hobie boards, but when Bob Head and Bill Bailey started producing lighter and more maneuverable boards under the Bilbo brand, Matthews found those boards better suited, and so he switched his allegiance to Bilbo. The board shown here is the fifth Bilbo he owned. Made in 1970, this board is 10 feet long. It has had a new fin added, and although it is discolored by sunlight, the board has character and still rides well, according to Matthews. "It is a classic of its time," he added. "I was never a fan of the shortboard era and remained faithful to the roots of British surfing and rode a locally made board."

Photo by Alex Williams; Board courtesy Stuart Matthews

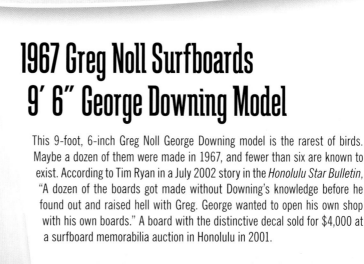

1967 Greg Noll Surfboards
9′ 6″ George Downing Model

This 9-foot, 6-inch Greg Noll George Downing model is the rarest of birds. Maybe a dozen of them were made in 1967, and fewer than six are known to exist. According to Tim Ryan in a July 2002 story in the *Honolulu Star Bulletin*, "A dozen of the boards got made without Downing's knowledge before he found out and raised hell with Greg. George wanted to open his own shop with his own boards." A board with the distinctive decal sold for $4,000 at a surfboard memorabilia auction in Honolulu in 2001.

Photos by Juliana Morais; Board courtesy Fernando Aguerre

GEORGE DOWNING
MODEL
Custom
GREG NOLL
Surfboards

Harbour 8′ 6″ Mini Baby Gun

When the shortboard revolution hit, Rich Harbour hired *Endless Summer* star Robert August to move the Harbour label into the future. But there was no panic in the shaping bays. "For me, I enjoy the challenge to work on designing newer and better-riding surfboards," Harbour said. "I was bummed that the Aussies were getting all the ink in the magazines. McTavish certainly was blazing new trails, but we were looking at his shorter stuff and making slight changes in the designs that we felt were improvements." The Baby Gun was an example of Harbour's understanding of surfboard design by 1968. But the Baby Gun design was short-lived, according to Harbour: "It was super stiff—not your choice for San Onofre at high tide and four foot. The logo, designed by former *Surfer* magazine art editor Leo Bestgen, is the best thing about the board."

Photo by Juliana Morais; Board courtesy Fernando Aguerre

1967 LSD 8' 6"

This 8-foot, 6-inch pintail miniature gun with Lewis Carroll-ish custom art was produced for Lahaina Surf Designs: LSD. Get it? Dick Brewer switched from Hobie to Harbour Surfboards in 1966 then went to Bing in 1967, where he produced the Pipeliner, the Lotus, the Pintail, and the Nuuhiwa Lightweight. But the shortboard revolution was bubbling, and after getting fired from Bing, Brewer was here today, gone to Maui. Lahaina placed Brewer close to the ultimate test track—Honolua Bay—and for one year, he was one of the major movers behind the mini-gun revolution. When Bob McTavish and Nat Young came to Maui with their Fantastic Plastic machines, Brewer met them with Reno Abellira and Gerry Lopez, and it was game on—to the benefit of everyone who would ride a surfboard from 1967 on.

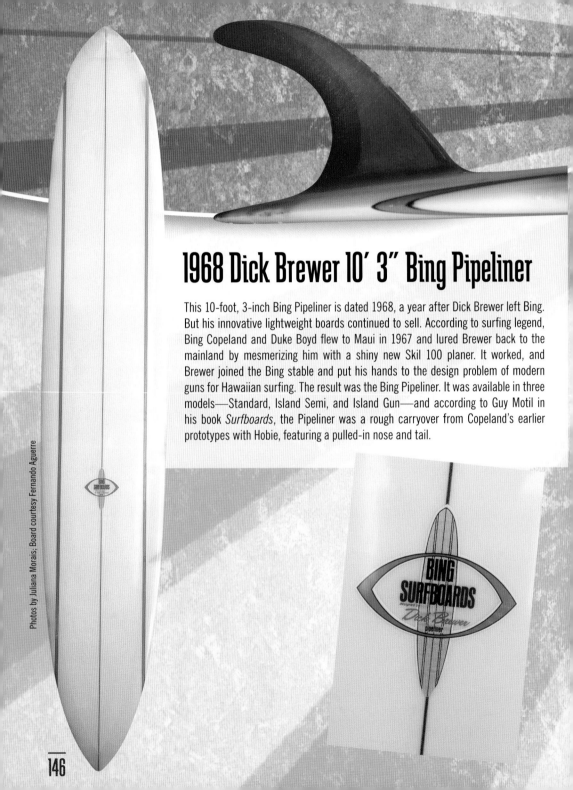

1968 Dick Brewer 10' 3" Bing Pipeliner

This 10-foot, 3-inch Bing Pipeliner is dated 1968, a year after Dick Brewer left Bing. But his innovative lightweight boards continued to sell. According to surfing legend, Bing Copeland and Duke Boyd flew to Maui in 1967 and lured Brewer back to the mainland by mesmerizing him with a shiny new Skil 100 planer. It worked, and Brewer joined the Bing stable and put his hands to the design problem of modern guns for Hawaiian surfing. The result was the Bing Pipeliner. It was available in three models—Standard, Island Semi, and Island Gun—and according to Guy Motil in his book *Surfboards*, the Pipeliner was a rough carryover from Copeland's earlier prototypes with Hobie, featuring a pulled-in nose and tail.

Morey-Pope Bob McTavish Tracker

Joe McGovern found this Morey-Pope Tracker board outside of Water Brothers surf shop in Newport, Rhode Island. It was designed and shaped by Bob McTavish, who contends that the Tracker was the first production shortboard. "Although it was only a foot shorter than the average Californian board," McTavish said, "it quickly tumbled into the succeeding foot-long discounting war of 1968 and '69. It was the first, being designed in January '68, and hitting the stores in February."

McTavish called the design a compromise between what he was riding at Rincon— sub-8-foot pointed nose (a la Brewer), barely any vee, classic speed shape—with what was being developed in Australia at the time—mid-8-foot vee bottom boards, as a more acceptable step-down transition design. According to McTavish, Morey-Pope had an eye on his Rincon board as the next release, but it never happened, as Tom Morey instead came out with the 1969 boards known as the Stradivarius and the Camel.

Photos by Joe McGovern

Mark Fragale's Hynson Red Fin

An avid collector and director of the Honolulu Surfing Museum (home to Jimmy Buffett's collection), Mark Fragale moved to Hawaii in 1970 and began a personal collection of 100 surfboards. He is especially fond of his Hynson red fin guns, of which only 8 or 12 were made, according to Fragale. He owns four redfins, one of which is the board that Mike Hynson rode in the inaugural Duke Kahanamoku Invitational Contest in 1965. These boards were produced only from late 1965 into 1966.

Fragale described the complex process for getting the red color of the fins: "The red color on the skegs was accomplished by running the center layup of the fin in white pigment and all the subsequent scheduled layers of glass in the near blood-red pigment. The white core layup prevented light from traveling through the otherwise somewhat translucent colored skegs of the era. The white center strip adds a hint of elegance to the finished product."

Photo by Elizabeth Pepin; Board courtesy Mark Fragale

1968 Dick Brewer Kauai 7' 4" Mini-Gun

The shortboard revolution also revolutionized big-wave guns. In the 1950s and '60s, long, heavy elephant guns were ridden by giant men, but by the early 1970s, surfboards were smaller, lighter, and sleeker, just as big-wave riders were smaller, lighter, and sleeker. For example, at the 1974 Smirnoff Pro/Am held in giant surf at Waimea Bay, Reno Abellira beat Jeff Hakman by a fraction of a point. But the point is, if Reno were sitting on Hakman's shoulders, those two combined (both Reno and Jeff were right around 5 feet, 6 or 7 inches and 130 to 140 pounds) would have just barely surpassed the height or weight of a Greg Noll (6 feet, 2 inches and 230 pounds) or the Thunder Lizards who had dominated the big surf on their elephant guns through the previous decades. This 7-foot, 4-inch Brewer mini-gun, from circa 1968, is proof of that evolution to smaller boards.

Photo by Greg Lui-Kwan

Farrer's Hyper-Kicked Nose

With the shortboard revolution's spirit of experimentation, things like nose scoop went to both extremes. At the 1968 World Contest in Puerto Rico, Reno Abellira rode *Le Serpent Plastique*, a 6-foot, 10-inch by 17-inch board that was 3 inches thick and had very flat rocker.

Reno and Dick Brewer went the other way with rocker in 1969, resulting in a hyper-kicked nose design called the Disc. According to Abellira in a 1969 ad, "The Disc is not pearl proof, but it saves me 90 percent of the time in crucial situations."

This late-1960s board with a hyper-kicked nose—proudly held by owner Cameron Farrer of Malibu—is somewhere between a duck-billed platypus and a Chinese aircraft carrier. Abellira said that neither he nor Brewer had anything to do with the creation of this board, beyond being the inspiration for it at some point. "Though they are rare," he added, "real ones exist do exist out there."

Photo by Lucia Griggi; Board courtesy Cameron Farrer

1968 Johnny Fain
Formula II 7-Footer

Some surfers—and surfboards—survived the transition into the shortboard revolution. Some didn't. In *The Encyclopedia of Surfing*, Matt Warshaw described Johnny Fain as a "fast-talking, whip-turning, regular-foot surfer from Malibu, California." Fain was a longboard hotdogger of the same school as Dewey Weber and Miki Dora; Fain and Dora had a great rivalry going at Malibu through the 1960s. As the shortboard revolution hit, Dora went off on his own adventures, while Fain came out with the Fain Formula model, produced by Greg Noll Surfboards. This 7-footer is a Fain Formula II, which Fain and many others used to put their foot on the tail and ride the pocket into the 1970s.

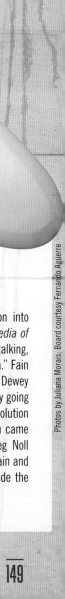

7' 7" Bilbo Rounded Pintail Double Ender

Collector Alex Williams dated this board—a 7-foot, 7-inch Bilbo rounded pintail shaped by Chris Jones—around 1968, and if that is true, then British surfboards were looking clean by then. Jones has been making epoxy boards since the late 1990s, but his website states that he started making surfboards in Newquay in 1965, "learning his trade in the old Bilbo factory in the 1960s." Jones was a competitive surfer and won the English, British, and European titles in the same year. He is also a former Cornish and British Junior champion.

Williams described the board as a "second generation CJ model/double ender, more pulled in in the tail, inspired by Young, Lynch, and Treloar, who we bumped into on a trip to Biarritz. Watching those guys surf [at] Lafitenia, Guethary, and La Barre was absolutely amazing—the best surfing any of us had seen to date."

Tiki 7' 6" Rounded Pin

This 7-foot, 6-inch by 21-inch by 2⅝-inch Tiki rounded pin, single fin comes from around 1968, when the shortboard revolution was inspiring an industrial revolution in the English surf-industrial complex. Tiki Surfboards has been based in Braunton, North Devon, since 1968, and longtime co-owner Dave Aldrich-Smith has a memory that goes back even further: "I blew the Castle blanks (and later Bennett) way back then. Keith Paull [1968 Australian Titles champ] came and shaped for a while in 1968–69 when we were in Abergavenny, Gwent—along with three South Africans who called in with 6-foot, 6-inch 'wunderboards.' They set the Gower beaches alight with their performances when all and sundry had 8-foot, 6-inch or longer boards." Aldrich-Smith believes this board could be one of Keith Paull's shapes, due to its distinctive design. The board decals from 1967 and '68 did not have the green frills along the edges, and according to Aldrich-Smith, the pictured decal ceased when they moved to Devon.

Photos by Alex Williams

151

1969 Greg Noll
7' 6" No-Nose

This Greg Noll "No Nose" board is from about 1969. This is the year Noll was the last man standing on a giant day at Makaha, a session he survived and which historians point to as the end of an era and the start of another. Within a couple of years, Noll would pack up his business and his family and move to northern California to reinvent himself as a commercial fisherman. But in 1969, Greg Noll Surfboards was going strong and this was a transitional board with a wide, round tail and a narrow, pulled-in, and flipped up "no nose." The board has no stringer and uses the Fins Unlimited Vari-Set fin system.

Photos by Juliana Morais; Board courtesy Fernando Aguerre

1969 Morey-Pope Sopwith Camel

The Sopwith Camel was a deadly accurate World War I British single-seat biplane fighter introduced in 1917; it was credited with shooting down 1,294 enemy planes. In the *Peanuts* cartoons, Snoopy fantasized about flying a Sopwith Camel against the Red Baron. The Sopwith Camel airplane was short, fast, and maneuverable, and perhaps that is why Morey-Pope named its 1969 shortboard revolution offering after the famous plane.

Photo by Lucia Griggi; Board courtesy John Mazza

Yater Hawaii 8′ 4″ Gun

John Mazza bought this Yater gun at the 2001 Hawaiian Islands Vintage Surf Auction. The brochure's description was terse: "Yater Surfboard Hawaii Model. 8′ 4″ 1969 team board with green inlay, rough deck, black rails, clear bottom, glass on fin. Designed to ride Hawaii with the rare Yater Hawaii laminate."

Photo by Lucia Griggi; Board courtesy John Mazza

Sid Abruzzi's Overlin Gun

The son of Rhode Island football legend Duke Abruzzi, Sid Abruzzi opened Water Brothers Surf Shop in Newport in 1971, and that shop became an epicenter for worldwide surf and skate culture. In 2011, Abruzzi was the driving force behind the Doris Duke Surf Fest, a vintage surfboard show held on the Rough Point estate of Doris Duke, an heiress who surfed with Duke Kahanamoku in the 1930s. Abruzzi has had hundreds and thousands of surfboards under his feet and in his hands over the decades. This one is

Photo by Joe McGovern; Board courtesy Sid Abruzzi

a 1969 gun made by Santa Cruz shaper Tom Overlin. Santa Cruz surfers from that era will recognize the five-pointed star, an ubiquitous emblem of Tracy's Fiberglass Works. "My first time to Santa Cruz was the fall of 1971," recalled Abruzzi, "and I've been going there every year ever since. . . . Back in the 1970s I became good friends with Tom and Jim Overlin, and over the years I have sold and ridden hundreds of their boards. This isn't one of the boards I rode. It's one I sold that came back to me in pristine condition, and I never let go of it for over 25 years."

Channin/Diffenderfer Balsa Gun

Born in Beverly Hills but raised in La Jolla, Mike Diffenderfer first rode a surfboard at 10 years old. Diffenderfer jumped to the North Shore in 1956 and teamed up with Tony Channin to make surfboards for Hawaii and California. Diffenderfer was the Hawaii arm, and he spent the next 25 years, mostly in Hawaii, surfing Makaha and the North Shore. He was on the beach the first time the Banzai Pipeline was ridden, and some say Diffenderfer put the "Pipeline" tag on the spot. Diffenderfer shaped his first board out of balsa in 1951. In 1969, he went back to the future to shape this 7-foot, 10-inch balsa mini-gun, made for Jimmy "The Impala" Lucas of Kauai. The board is now in the collection of John Mazza who said, "This is one of only six balsas made by Mike Diffenderfer during the transition era. . . . There are unique slits along the rail line to try get more nose rocker—17 inches wide and very advanced for its time. It required a surfer with the skill of Jimmy Lucas to ride it because of its narrowness and radical design for the time."

Board and photos courtesy John Mazza/Pepperdine University

Jock Sutherland's Personal Plastic Fantastic

This 7-foot, 7-inch Plastic Fantastic mini-gun was the personal surfboard of Jock Sutherland. According to the Stoked 'n Board website, the company name was inspired by the Jefferson Airplane song "Plastic Fantastic Lover." The company began producing surfboards in 1968 on the North Shore of Oahu and in Huntington Beach. Plastic Fantastic was one of the most popular labels in the 1970s.

Jock shaped the board himself, and he remembers it well. "One thing that's interesting," he said, "it was fairly narrow and under 18 inches. I wanted a board that was 18.5 inches or 19 inches, but I shaped one rail and tried too hard to make it perfect. I thought I had overdone it and made it too skinny, but because of the nose and rail and vee—it ended up working out. I rode it at Pipe, Haleiwa, Pupukea."

Kevin Miller at the Pepperdine library did measure this at 18 inches at its widest point. So this is Jock's functional mistake, going back to 1969.

Board and photos courtesy John Mazza/Pepperdine University

1969 6' 8" Weber Ski

Check out Paul Witzig's *The Hot Generation* (1971), and there's Nat Young putting his Weber Ski through its paces, looking thoroughly modern carving turns in the pocket, pulling into the tube and doing big, smooth cutbacks. "Made it in France," Nat Young said. "Took it to Puerto Rico for the World Champs. Weber came and did the production as I went back to Oz. The first plastic fins went on all the boards. They did not work at all."

According to Matt Warshaw in *The Encyclopedia of Surfing*, the shortboard revolution of the late 1960s was disastrous for Weber, as it was for many of the big-name surfboard manufacturers of the time. The big boys couldn't keep up with the constant changes in board design, and while Weber introduced the Young-designed streamlined Ski model in 1969, the business never recovered from the transition, and by 1973 Weber Surfboards was reduced to a single factory and retail outlet in Hermosa Beach.

Photos by Juliana Morais; Board courtesy Fernando Aguerre

Larry Balma's Homemade Boards

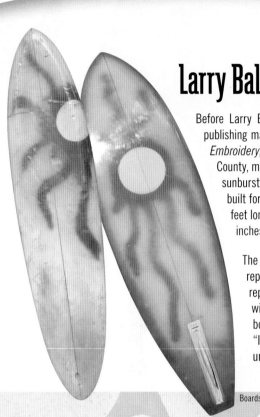

Before Larry Balma was a skateboard mogul (Tracker Trucks) and a publishing magnate (*Trans World Skate*, *Trans World Surf*, *Trans World Embroidery*, et al.), he was a hippie surfer dude in North San Diego County, making boards for himself and his kin. The board with the full sunburst painted on the bottom was the first surfboard that Balma built for his daughter when she was five years old in 1970. It is 5 feet long, 14 inches wide at the nose, 17 inches midpoint, and 12 inches at the tail. The color is airbrushed foam.

The board painted with the three-quarters sunburst is the replica of Balma's own 1969 board; both the original and the replica were shaped by Dickie Pierce. It is 7 feet, 6 inches with a 21½-inch midpoint. "I had never seen any other boards airbrushed when I was doing these," Balma recalled. "I have no idea if I was first—never really thought about it until now."

Boards and photos courtesy Larry Balma

Tom Morey's Experimental 9-Step Air Induction Board

Tom Morey received a B.A. in mathematics from the University of Southern California in 1957 and then went to work for Douglas Aircraft as a process engineer in composites. In 1964 he left the corporate world and entered the surf world, and he has been experimenting ever since. Dating from the early 1970s, this 6-foot, 10-inch Tom Morey Experimental 9-Step Air Induction Board was sold at the 2005 Hawaiian Islands Vintage Surf Auction. According to the auction brochure, it was one of Morey's "monumental steps in the direction of 'air-lubricated' designs. Featuring air induction deck holes, nine steps with fiberglass, Filon-sheet, hard-edge planing areas, removable fin. Deck features double pinlines, with progressive round tail design."

Photo by Lucia Griggi; Board courtesy John Mazza.

Evo Replica of Wayne Lynch's 7′ 10″ *Evolution* Board

In 2000, Wayne Lynch shaped 50 limited-edition replicas (40 in Australia, 10 in America) of the board he rode to change the world circa 1968, a revolution shown in living color in the movie *Evolution*.

Wayne Lynch got a Plastic Machine from Bob McTavish in 1967, and it soon inspired Lynch to start shaping his own boards. The original board on which this replica is based was the fourth board ever shaped by Lynch. "Everything was changing so rapidly," he recalled, "that two months seemed like years in terms of the difference in design. We often went to extremes trying to find out the possibilities of a particular concept. I shaped the first one in the summer of '67. In '68, when it fell apart, I tried to copy it exactly, as I loved it so much. I shaped this one in Easter of 1968, and this is the board that's on the poster for the *Evolution* film. The first one and this were the boards that let my surfing develop and do the turns up the face, etc." The board was 7 feet, 10 inches long and had its wide point about 6 inches behind center. It was very thin and had a very subtle vee and flat sections in the bottom shape.

Photos by Juliana Morais; Board courtesy Fernando Aguerre

John Conway's 6' 2" "Economy" Model

The Brits truly made some lovely surfboards back in the day. Produced circa 1971, this 6-foot, 2-inch by 21-inch rounded pintail was produced by John Conway and was called the Economy board, as it sold for £33-19-11d, as opposed to the deluxe version. Using rough exchange and inflation rates, that translates to about $450 in modern money, when shortboards regularly sell for $600 to $1,000.

Economics aside, John Conway was a stalwart member of the UK surfing community who passed away at age 55 in March 2003. He was an early member of the surf scene, shaping hundreds of surfboards as he traveled the world. His passion for photography led to Conway setting up a studio, and in the summer of 1981, he published the first issue of *Wavelength Surfing* magazine.

Photo by Alex Williams

Steve Barger's Auga Friction-Free Board

John Mazza said this black beast is an Auga board, a 1970s phenomenon that still resonates today with Boogie Boards and the friction-free set. The Auga came from Bing Copeland making boards for surfers in the South Bay of Los Angeles who wanted to surf after the lifeguards hoisted the Black Ball flag at 10:00— no surfboards allowed. "Bing and Mike Eaton began messing around with a reject blank," explained Mazza, "and they came up with a short, finless board with a deep channel in the rear that could be ridden after the beach closed because it did not have fins. They called it 'Flying Nun' after Sally Fields's hat. Bing had a couple of team riders test it out and they pronounced it unrideable, so it sat in the shop for a while. . . . Sometime later Steve Barger came along and took an interest. He realized there was too much 'grab' for such a short board and reshaped the design into an Auga. The black Auga board was Steve Barger's. He became Auga Man."

Tom Morey's Soft-Skinned Auga

The Auga board is essentially the 1970s version of the "friction-free" boards that are popular with experimenters in the 21st century. This Auga was designed by Tom Morey, and it married Auga design with soft technology from the early 1970s. It was sold at the 2005 Hawaiian Islands Vintage Surf Auction, which described its "'Auga' channel bottom, twin-fin set up, soft shell skin. Deck structural inserts, with-or-without twin-fin set up. All the applications way ahead of their time!"

The final design of the Auga board was two flat planing surfaces on either side of a channel running down the back end on the bottom, providing lift and enough release that the board would not "grab." The deck side had a raised surface on it similar to the bottom of a Kelly Hydro. While this may look like a bellyboard, it was intended for standup surfing.

Gerry Lopez's 1971 Auga Bolt

When the Auga boards came to Maui in the early 1970s, they caught the eye of Gerry Lopez. According to John Mazza, the current owner of this board, Lopez shaped this yellow and orange Auga for Tom Warren. "[Lopez] and John Porter considered producing them out of soft material about the time Tom Morey came up with the prototype soft Auga-like board that had detachable fins," explained Mazza. "The result of that prototype was Morey drifting off to invent the soft boogie board."

Photos by Lucia Griggi; Board courtesy John Mazza

Nat Young's 6′ 4″ Rounded Pin

Nat Young shaped this 6-foot, 4-inch somewhat rounded pintail at Byron Bay in 1970 or 1971. Many years later, he inscribed that fact on the tail of the board—the same tail where Nat so famously placed his XXL right foot and continued to change the surfing world into the 1970s. After winning the World Championship at Ocean Beach, San Diego in 1966, Young starred in a number of surf movies, including *Morning of the Earth* and *The Hot Generation*. He was part of the mini-gun push in Hawaii in 1967, and in 1969, he co-starred with Wayne Lynch in *Evolution*. A year later, he was a featured surfer in George Greenough's *Crystal Voyager*— all 6 feet, 3 inches, 185 pounds of him flying up, in, and around the curl at stormy, hollow Rincon on a shortboard. He went on to be a multi-time winner of the Longboard World Championships.

Mike Hynson's Far Out 8-Footer

This clean 8-footer was made circa 1970 by Mike Hynson. The clean-cut star of *The Endless Summer*, Hynson survived the shortboard revolution and became one of the innovators of the mini-gun. Herbie Fletcher, who was also involved in California and Hawaii, called Hynson "The Maharishi." Fletcher said that when the shortboard revolution arrived, Hynson was a "damned good surfer. He was very innovative, and he would go out and surf with all those guys and shape surfboards. Our surfboards started out at Backdoor I think around 8 feet, 6 inches, you know. The mini-guns started and then they went down to 8 feet, 2 inches and 7 feet, 9 inches, and they kept on going down."

Gerry Lopez took a look at his board and believes it was either one of Hynson's own or may have been made for one of the members of the Brotherhood of Eternal Love, a group of Orange County surfers who began as a commune but were involved in trafficking psychedelic drugs and hashish, among other legendary activities. Whomever the board was made for, Lopez noted that Hynson used the "down rail" before anybody else, in lieu of the tucked under edge. "This single feature may have been, besides the reduction in length and volume, the most telling single factor in making the shortboard a totally functional surf vehicle."

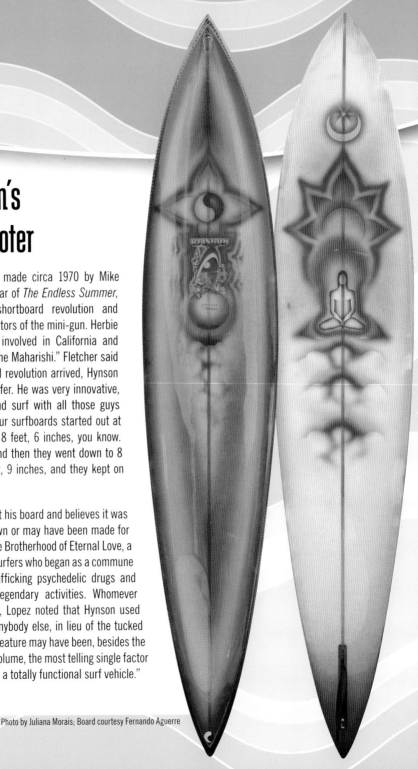

Photo by Juliana Morais; Board courtesy Fernando Aguerre

Koniakowsky and Hynson's *Grace*

Named for his mother, the *Grace* model developed through three versions in about 1973 or 1974 under the hand of Mike Hynson; this one found its way back into Hynson's hands many years later. In 2012, when Wade Koniakowsky went looking for a board-canvas for the Board Art Benefit for Surf Aid, he approached Hynson, who felt strongly that the surviving *Grace* model should be the board. Koniakowsky wanted to impart an overall psychedelic feel to represent the era of many of Hynson's designs, and what better symbol than Jimi Hendrix. "The fin is the Hynson designed 'DOL-FIN' based on the dorsal fin of a dolphin," said Koniakowsky, "thus the dolphins circling Hendrix. The art is completed with the 'wahine mermaids' with variegated gold tail sections, swirling kelp and seahorses."

Koniakowsky and Hynson's *Rainbow Bridge*

A second Mike Hynson board that Wade Koniakowsky painted for the 2012 Board Art Benefit for Surf Aid tied into the 1972 movie *Rainbow Bridge*, a psychedelic counterculture film that included the last U.S. concert by Jimi Hendrix, held on the slopes of Haleakala, Maui, before an audience of a few hundred island hippies and surfers. Even though the concert connected to the movie of that name was in 1970, the board celebrating it more likely dates from 1973 or '74. The board was designed specifically to ride Maalaea, a wave on Maui that requires a very precise, giant south swell to break, so it breaks only rarely. But when it does, Maalaea is one of the fastest waves in the world.

Boards courtesy Wade Koniakowsky

Mike Tabeling's *Pacific Vibrations* Weber Ski

East Coaster Mike Tabeling was one of the stars of *Pacific Vibrations*, a 1970 surf movie made by *Surfer* magazine founder John Severson, and this was his board. The Weber Ski was shaped by Harold Iggy one week before the filming of the scene at the Hollister Ranch, north of Santa Barbara. The board has a slight vee, rounded pin, turned down tail rails, 50/50 nose rails, and a slight belly. "Ninety-nine percent of Dewey's Skis were run through his primitive shaping machine in Marina Del Rey," said Tabeling. "This one wasn't." Tabeling's artwork on the deck, and the resin acid-splash on the bottom, reflects the psychedelic 1970s perfectly: Jim Morrison and Mick Jagger drawn with pen and ink. "I did it over several nights in Carolyn and Dewey's back bedroom."

Jo Jo Perrin's 7′ 11″ Balsa Gun

This 7-foot, 11-inch balsa gun was shaped circa 1970 by Jo Jo Perrin, a Malibu surfer and shaper who first gained attention for his surprising performance at the 1964 Malibu Invitational Surfing Contest as a 14 year old. He was a member of Dewey Weber's surf team, along with Jackie Baxter, Joey Hamasaki, David Nuuhiwa, Mike Tabeling, and Nat Young. Perrin shaped a lot of experimental boards in the late 1960s, during the transitional period from longboards to shortboards. According to the John Mazza Historical Surfboard Collection at Pepperdine University, this balsa board may have been cut down from an older Pacific Systems Homes—type board, as suggested by the three dowels across the top. "This board also illustrates Perrin's artistic talent, which he applied to decorating his surfboards, often with mystical images and symbols."

Board and photos courtesy John Mazza/Pepperdine University

Bird's Caster/
Warner Balsa Board

If you love surfboards and you haven't been to Bird's Surf Shed in San Diego—well, stop denying yourself. Located within the pleasing, functional shape of a 100-by-40-foot Quonset hut, Bird's Surf Shed is a surf shop plus. "It's a retail store that also showcases a large amount of my personal collection," said Eric "Bird" Huffman. "Many of these boards [are] available to ride." Here Bird poses with his favorite among the 400 boards, a late-1970s, 7-foot, 6-inch-long by 19¾-inch-wide by 2⅝-inch-thick balsa single fin. Bill Caster started the board, hesitantly, with balsa that Bird hand-picked from a supply brought up from Ecuador. Caster didn't like mowing balsa, and the board wasn't finished until the early 1980s. Before Caster passed away from cancer in 1987, he suggested that his brother-in-law Hank Warner put the finishing touches on the shaped blank. This is the pride of Bird's many-feathered flock.

Photos by Lucia Griggi

Hendy and Harber 6' 6" Diamond Tail

This lovely 6-foot, 6-inch diamond tail shines out like a piece of lacquered fine jewelry, and it comes from the place Shakespeare described as "this sceptred isle . . . this precious stone set in the silver sea." England, in other words. According to Alasdair Lindsay of Vintage Surfboard Collector UK, Hendy and Harber was a small but important maker from about 1969 to 1971. Rob Hendy and Aussie lifeguard Tom "Buttercup" Holt were head shapers; Graham Nile was the team rider. They made about 200 boards (no longboards) in 6- to 8-foot lengths, most with Bilbo fin systems. The standard of finish was high, the boards were well made and glassed, but not many examples turn up. Hendy is now a successful performing magician and member of the Magic Circle, but he remembers his shaping days with pride.

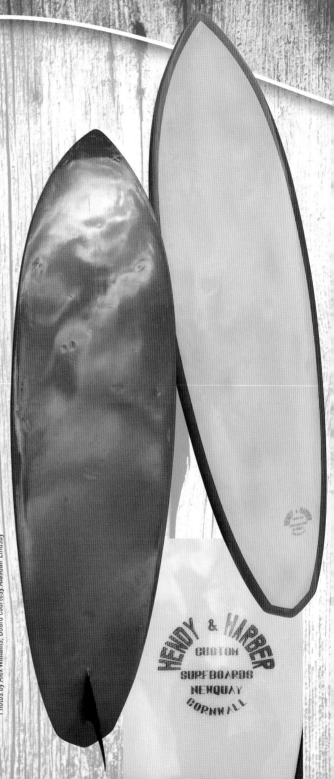

Photos by Alex Williams; Board courtesy Alasdair Lindsay

HENDY & HARBER CUSTOM SURFBOARDS NEWQUAY CORNWALL

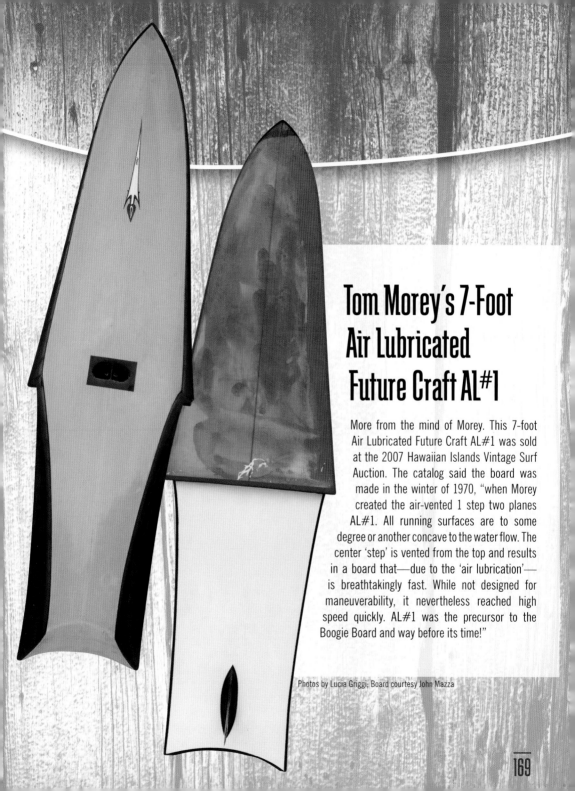

Tom Morey's 7-Foot Air Lubricated Future Craft AL#1

More from the mind of Morey. This 7-foot Air Lubricated Future Craft AL#1 was sold at the 2007 Hawaiian Islands Vintage Surf Auction. The catalog said the board was made in the winter of 1970, "when Morey created the air-vented 1 step two planes AL#1. All running surfaces are to some degree or another concave to the water flow. The center 'step' is vented from the top and results in a board that—due to the 'air lubrication'— is breathtakingly fast. While not designed for maneuverability, it nevertheless reached high speed quickly. AL#1 was the precursor to the Boogie Board and way before its time!"

Photos by Lucia Griggi; Board courtesy John Mazza

Photo by Joe McConey; Board courtesy Pete Pan

1971 Hobie Greg Loehr Seaboard

There are a whole lot of modern hipsters getting all retro on single-fin, diamond-tailed replicas of boards that go back to original art like this 1971 Hobie Seaboard, designed by Greg Loehr. This East Coast surfboard-materials pioneer was a top 1A amateur surfer at the beginning of 1971 and rose to number two in 4A at the end of the year, riding a Hobie. Fellow East Coast surf legend Gary Propper offered Loehr a Hobie model of his own, and the Seaboard was the result, designed and shaped as a cooperation between Greg Loehr and Terry Martin.

Pete Pan has been the proud owner of that orange Seaboard since the early 1970s, a hookup from Gary Propper during a Hobie team trip to Rhode Island. Propper had recruited Pan to join the Hobie team, with whom Pan made his first trip to Florida. "Gary Propper said to come visit him at the Ron Jon shop in Cocoa Beach," Pan recalled, "and he would set me up with a great contest board. That was the board. I even have shots of me and my wife with the board from the trip, and surfing on it later that month in Rhode Island."

Vinny Bryan 7′ 6″ Futuristic Air Board

This Vinny Bryan 7-foot, 6-inch Futuristic Surfboard sold for the far out price of $2,000 at Randy Rarick's 2001 Hawaii surf auction. According to the brochure: "Vinny shaped for an eclectic group of riders including Bunker Spreckels, who took his boards to new highs. Circa early 1970s. No question, this is the most advanced, trippy 70s board on offer! Full space model."

Bryan called the mainland from over the horizon and explained that he first visited Kauai in 1969 and is still on that island. Among the Kauai crew at that time was Bunker Spreckels, heir to the Spreckels sugar fortune and stepson to Clark Gable. Bunker was one of the most flamboyant characters of the surf scene in the late 1960s and early '70s. Bryan and others were living under Spreckels's house and experimenting with all kinds of things, including surfboards. Bryan made this board around 1972 or 1973 for a surfer named Todd Value. Bryan shaped it, but another artist did the color. He also made one for Spreckels. They called them Air Boards, but they were hard to ride because they sank. But Bryan rode big Hanalei on an Air Board that he claims was faster than anything else in the water.

Photo by Juliana Morais; Board courtesy Fernando Aguerre

Scott Bass's 5' 4" Lis Fish

One of Scott Bass's immortal beloveds, the genre of this 5-foot, 4-inch Lis Fish was described by Matt Warshaw in *The Encyclopedia of Surfing* as a "stumpy, blunt-nosed, two-finned surfboard design invented by San Diego kneeboarder Steve Lis in 1967, featuring low rocker and a split-tail, and later adapted for stand-up surfing."

Cher Pendarvis wrote the book on Steve Lis—well not the book, but a solid story in *The Surfer's Journal* called "Home Grown: Steve Lis and His Fish." Asked about this board in particular, Pendarvis described it as a sleek, racy example of a Lis kneeboard Fish. "This Lis Fish has a more pointed nose, more curve in the template and a narrower tail than most of Stevie's Fish from the early 1970s. It's likely that he shaped this Fish for larger, hollow waves (possibly Hawaii). . . . Most of his Fish from the early 1970s had wider noses and were wider pin to pin, with a straighter accelerating template toward the tail."

Steve Lis's Personal Lis Fish

This is Steve Lis's personal Fish, photographed at Sunset Cliffs in 2005. According to Lis scholar Cher Pendarvis, Lis shaped this 5-foot, 2-inch by 21½-inch Fish kneeboard for bigger waves in 1969–1970. He used a stringerless blank with a reverse-style layup, and an opaque apricot pigment on the deck, wrapping around to the bottom. The bottom is light gold pigment. Steve made the fin lay-up sheet and the fins too, which are based on his early keel template. The keels are double-foiled clear fiberglass, which was the material of choice before wood keel fins were made. This Fish was designed by Lis as a big-wave kneeboard, with a wide point forward template with an accelerating curve toward the tail. Its full, rounded nose with small point is a hallmark of early Fish designs. It measures 14 inches from pin to pin. The thickness is fairly even, and it has a clean foil and flat rocker. Lis said this is about the twelfth Fish that he made.

Bird Huffman's Plantain

"This is a good one!" said Bird Huffman, and we believed him. Bird explained that this Plantain was shaped by Steve Lis in 1971 for Bird's older brother Rex. A 5-foot kneeboard from the early years of the Fish, it has a round nose, stringerless blank, and glass keel fins and has a very flat rocker. This was the first board that Steve shaped for Rex, and it has always remained in the Huffman family. "Rex rode this board for many years," Bird said. "And the barrels it has seen at Big Rock, Blacks, Pipeline—you know it has clocked in some serious tube time. A true timepiece that looks like it does from many years in service long before leashes were invented."

Photos by Chris Park; Board courtesy Bird Huffman

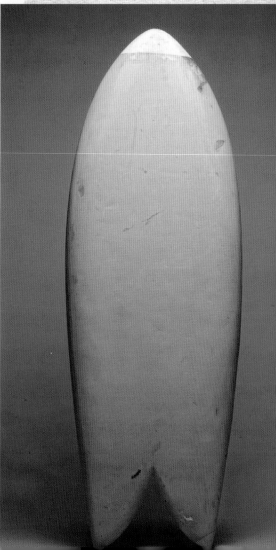

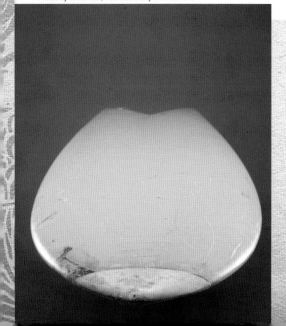

Yancy Spencer
MODEL

Hobie Yancy Spencer Model

Gulf Florida, represent! Perhaps best known for his presence in the surf industry and community along the Gulf Coast, Yancy Spencer opened Innerlight Surf Shop in 1972 in Gulf Breeze, a small town near Pensacola. In the years that followed, Innerlight expanded to include several locations in the surrounding area, which still serve as a gathering place for local wave riders. Hobie had done well with the Gary Propper model from Miami to Maine, and most likely they hoped to do the same from southwest Florida to South Padre Island with the Yancy Spencer model. This board belongs to Pete Pan, who got it from his neighbor, who originally got it from The Watershed shop in 1983. "I was always friends with Yancy," Pan said, "and whenever I surfed against him, he was always a gentleman in the water. It is a simple story: Hobie put the board out, Yancy wanted more money, no more boards made. The run only lasted a couple of months, maybe two."

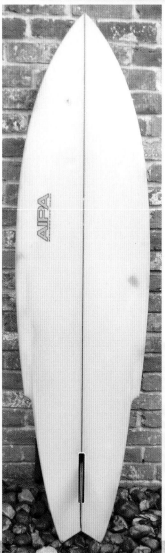

1972 Ben Aipa Stinger

The Stinger is a small-wave surfboard created in 1974 by Hawaiian surfer Ben Aipa. It was a hybrid that grafted the narrow tail section of a big-wave board onto the wider hips and nose of a small-wave hotdog board. The Stinger was ridden to great effect by the likes of Buttons Kaluhiokalani, Larry Bertlemann, and Mark Liddell in the 1970s.

This Stinger came from Jim and Mark Troutman by way of Michael Craydon. They bought the board in about 2003 from an ad in a local swap sheet from an owner who didn't know what he had and just wanted a few bucks for it. "The board has been a favorite rider in our transition board side of the collection and works well here in bigger Texas swell," Jim Troutman said. "We are big guys and love the full front end for the float. Aipa knew how to make a short board for big people." The board came with the matching Rainbow fin and remains in near-mint condition.

Photos by Jim and Mark Troutman, courtesy www.thesurfboardproject.com

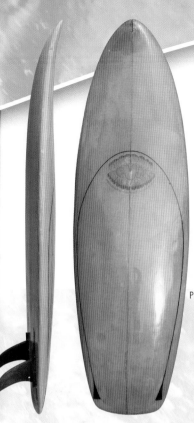

Stephen Harewood's Freedom Fun Machine

Those English types continued making quality surfboards into the 1970s. This 5-foot, 9-inch by 22½-inch Freedom Fun Machine was made by Stephen Harewood, who said it was designed in about 1971 to beat the "no-boards-over-six-feet" rules at Saint Brelades Bay in Jersey. "It was a Beachguards Buster," Harewood said. Current owner Alex Williams said the board was originally made for Jersey resident Gerry George.

Photos by Alex Williams

John Hall 7′ 2″ Swallowtail

This 7-foot, 2-inch by 19½-inch teardrop/swallow tail is 3 inches thick up at the front half of the board. The swallowtail and suction cup leash plug scream 1970s—like a revving GTO or Ozzy Osbourne singing "Iron Man."

This 1970s special was shaped by John Hall, who grew up in Sydney, Australia, and was in the same school year as Nat Young. He started shaping professionally after moving to South Africa in 1969 and then settled in Devon, England, a few years later. He became one of the top shapers for Tiki through the 1970s, and he also made a few of his own boards, such as this one. By the early 1980s he got into the windsurfing craze and was shaping them. Alex Williams has done a bit of screaming on this board: "I love surfing this board at Bantham when it has lined up long walls. A little step forward and it flies down the line."

Photo by Alex Williams

1973 Ocean Magic 6′ 4″ Wing-Swallow Twin Fin

Another early 1970s beauty from the United Kingdom, this 6-foot, 4-inch by 21-inch Ocean Magic wing-swallowtail twin fin was shaped by Peter "Moony" McAllum for Steve Daniel, according to Alex Williams. Daniel competed in the 1978 Worlds in South Africa and brought back MR twin fins, which he rode for the next year. Then "Moony" McAllum made this first twin fin for Daniel, and after riding it for some time he moved down in size from 6 feet 4 inches. The board was featured on the cover of the very first edition of *Wavelength Magazine* in 1981, with Steve Daniel surfing the World Contest in France in 1980.

Photos by Alex Williams

The Bonzer 1970

At the dawn of the 1970s, Duncan and Malcolm Campbell from Ventura, California, developed a three-finned board with channels that they called the Bonzer—which is Australian slang for "good" or "bitchin'." They built their first board in November 1970 using a 5-foot, 4-inch kneeboard shaped from a Clark Foam reject blank. The middle fin was big and boxy and placed well back on a squash-tail; the side fins were long, plastic blades put well forward of the middle fin.

In early 1973, they took the board to Bing Copeland and his head shaper Mike Eaton, and they made a deal that paid two dollars a board. Bing hyped the Bonzer with magazine ads, and the board lived up to the hype when Ian Cairns rode one to victory at the 1973 Smirnoff Contest at Laniakea.

Bing sold out to Gordon & Smith Surfboards in 1974, which detoured the popularity of the design. But the Bonzer is still up there on the Mount Rushmore of surfboard design. "We championed the three-fin cause for ten years before the world caught on with Simon's Thruster," Duncan Campbell told Steve Barilotti. "But it came true. Nobody can say that three-fins didn't become the best high-performance surfboards."

Author's collection

At the 2008 Sacred Craft Show in Del Mar, California, the "Bonzer Brotherhood"—(left to right) Duncan Campbell, Tom Moss (the board's owner), Malcolm Campbell, and Bing Copeland—pose with a 7-foot, 6-inch Bonzer, #8076, that was shaped by Copeland in 1973. The board has a yellow tinted deck and blue "Color Flo" fiberglass inlay on the bottom.

Mark Richards' *Free Ride* Twin Fin

On his blog, Mark Richards is not reticent about proclaiming the importance of what he calls his *"Free Ride* twin fins": "These are two of the most important boards in surfing history!!! You can call me an ego-maniac but it is a fact." Richards's re-invention of the twin fin changed surfing history and the perception of what high-performance surfing meant. This revolutionary design virtually killed the single fin as the board of choice in small surf. Richards reveals that there were actually two *Free Ride* twin fins: one 6-foot, 4-inch by 2-inches by 2⅞ inches, which was the board Richards rode, and a back-up board that was 6-foot, 6-inches by 20¼ inch by 2⅞-inch. The narrower second board was designed for bigger surf, but Richards rode the 6-foot, 4-inch in most conditions. His secret weapon sent others searching for their secret weapons. "My breakaway competitive success on the twin fin inspired other surfer/shapers to come up with something to try to stop me," Richards said. "Hence Simon's redo of the Thruster."

Photos by Juliana Morais; Board courtesy Fernando Aguerre

Tiki 6' 10" Diamond Tail

The United Kingdom making the 1970s look clean—if a little yellow. Dave Aldrich-Smith said that this 6-foot, 10-inch by 19½-inch Surfboards Great Britain diamond-tail was one of the first that John Hall shaped. Aldrich-Smith blew all the Dion blanks then (formulae courtesy of Barry Bennet, Australia) with up to eight concrete molds. The leash cups and fin boxes were fiberglass-molded by someone on England's south coast who was a pattern maker/craftsman for the Concorde superstructure.

"The board looks in extremely good nick [condition]," said Aldrich-Smith. "The name came from Floyd Smith of Gordon & Smith. He had just started Surfboards Australia and called in to check us out with the G&S franchise Tiki had at the time. It may have had 1974 on the lifeguard sticker, but quite a few were made in '72 and '73."

Photos by Alex Williams

Courtesy Alex Williams

Larry Strada's 8-Foot Hanalei Balsa

In the early 1970s, Larry Strada was one of the surfboard shapers who'd taken the Haj to Kauai, to ride perfect waves in one of the most beautiful spots on the planet—and perfect his shaping abilities. Strada was a co-founder of Lahaina Surf Designs (LSD) with Buddy Boy in the spring of 1968. This 8-foot by 17½-inch balsa board was made circa 1974. Because balsa wood feels alive, the medium never died for some shapers and surfers. "I got this balsa gun from my cousin Francis Kealoha, who lives on Kauai, who got it from Tommy Chambers," said current owner Greg Lui-Kwan. "In the mid-70s, Francis took this board around the world surfing Jeffrey's Bay in South Africa with touring professional surfers."

Two Richardson-Brewer Speedy Beauties

These circa-1975 Brewer's Beauties are a 7-foot, 5-inch pintail (the yellow one) and a 7-foot, 7-inch swallowtail (the blue one). The present owner of these boards, Greg Lui-Kwan, was jazzed to be connected with the shaper of these boards. "Of the 1970s Brewer shapers," Lui-Kwan said. "I like the Sam Hawks and Jim Richardsons the best."

Originally from Santa Cruz, Jim Richardson learned to shape with Doug Haut in the late 1960s. He spent most of the 1970s shaping on the North Shore with Dick Brewer Surfboards and later Local Motion. He now teaches entrepreneurship at the University of Hawaii and runs Surflight Hawaii, which manufactures a unique high-tech high performance soft surfboard with enhanced flex. Richardson said that one of the cool things about working with Brewer was that he got several templates from him, and these boards were from his early years with Brewer. "You have to remember that we only had one fin back there," Richardson said, "so the tails had to be pretty narrow to hold at Pipe or Sunset. We loosened them up with rocker and rail foils (a seemingly lost art). The wide points look deceptively far forward. If you look carefully, they are actually just slightly ahead of center. Getting that wide point blend right was something I learned from Brewer. You could be way forward and burying the rail and nothing would catch or push."

Zuma Jay's 7-Foot Balsa Board

Jefferson "Zuma Jay" Wagner has worn many hats in his day: a cowboy hat as the Marlboro Man in the 1980s, an LA County sheriff's hat in the 1990s, and a safety helmet and protective goggles as a top stuntman, FX, and pyrotechnic man in Hollywood. Zuma Jay was also the mayor of a small, prosperous California town, and he served on the Malibu City Council from 2008 to 2012. But going back to the 1970s, Jay wore the furrowed brow of a small business owner when he opened Zuma Jay's Surf Shop in 1975.

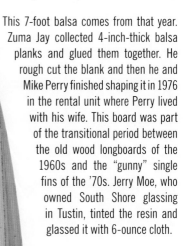

This 7-foot balsa comes from that year. Zuma Jay collected 4-inch-thick balsa planks and glued them together. He rough cut the blank and then he and Mike Perry finished shaping it in 1976 in the rental unit where Perry lived with his wife. This board was part of the transitional period between the old wood longboards of the 1960s and the "gunny" single fins of the '70s. Jerry Moe, who owned South Shore glassing in Tustin, tinted the resin and glassed it with 6-ounce cloth.

Photos by Lucia Griggi; Board courtesy John Mazza

Skip Frye Cyrious Egg

A close look at this Egg found the word "Cyrious." Thought that might be for Cyrus Sutton, but that was a dead end. Bird Huffman gave the scoop. This Frye 6-foot, 10-inch single fin Egg was built in 1974 or '75 and shaped out behind San Diego's Select Surf Shop. The board was glassed locally by one of the boys and custom built for Marl Cyr—hence the Cyrious reference on the stringer. "One of the cleanest examples of a Skip Frye Egg in terms of shape that I have ever seen," Bird said.

Jo Jo Perrin's Birthday Swallowtail

According to John Mazza, this 6-foot, 2½-inch swallowtail was made in 1977 for former Malibu local Chuck Walker as a present from Jo Jo Perrin on Chuck's tenth birthday. The deck is inscribed with the following poem.

> Little one looking at all to see.
> Growing strong and growing free.
> You wonder. . .
> Of the thunder
> Beyond the great sea
> You wonder why we can't be
> Living and giving in simplicity
> The cost of living
> Begins with giving
> Give your love
> And paint your dreams
> Aginst (sic) tomorrows
> Endless scenes
> Make them good
> As good as you will
> Think of a tree of wood
> As you walk the hill.

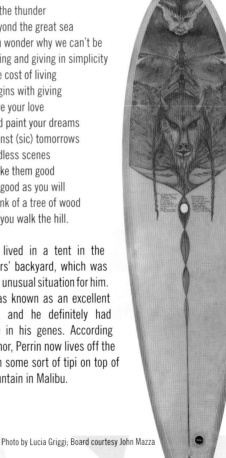

Jo Jo lived in a tent in the Walkers' backyard, which was not an unusual situation for him. He was known as an excellent artist, and he definitely had hippie in his genes. According to rumor, Perrin now lives off the grid in some sort of tipi on top of a mountain in Malibu.

Tommy Nellis 10' 3" Gator Gun

This 10-foot, 3-inch Tom Nellis Lightning Bolt "Outside Gator" gun was made for Outside Alligators, an outer reef west of Waimea, infamous for drowning Oahu big-wave surfer Todd Chesser in the 1990s. In the late 1970s, Outside Alligators was a big, forbidding peak on the horizon that began to pop when Waimea Bay was breaking. Back when the only way to catch these waves was with your bare arms, Tommy Nellis and others were shaping "Gator Guns" for hunting down horizon-breaking reptiles. Nellis made this board on Oahu and shipped it to Maui, where local boy Matt Kinoshita rode it at an outer reef known as Pier One. Nellis took the board back, and it went out to Outside Alligators, but not under Nellis's feet. "The range for those Outside Alligators boards started at 10 feet 3 inches, and I think I made a couple of 11-footers," said Nellis. "Outside Alligators is a really, really big field. You had to have a lot of paddle power and what we call 'penetrator rocker' because paddling was at least as important as riding. It's easy to get caught inside out there, and if you did you were really in trouble."

Board and photos courtesy John Mazza/Pepperdine University

John Porter's
8′ 5″ Tommy Nellis Bolt

Tommy Nellis shaped this 8-foot, 5-inch gun for John Porter, a good surfer and nice guy who used it on Maui at Honolua Bay, Hookipa, and a secret left reef called Pakakala. Nellis was born in Panama to a military family that moved around, and then Nellis moved himself to Hawaii around 1971. Mentored by Tom Eberly, Nellis was 18 or 19 when he was welcomed to the Lightning Bolt boutique around 1974. "It was an honor to work for Lightning Bolt," Nellis said. "It was a very democratic place. They would accept your boards as long as they were accepted by the public. If your boards didn't sell, it didn't matter who you were. They appreciated consistency, and at that time in the surfboard business it was easy to be consistent." When asked if a Tommy Nellis surfboard had ever done something substantial, Nellis said: "Yeah, I won the Haleiwa Surfing Championship. I think it was in 1978."

Board and photos courtesy John Mazza/Pepperdine University

Bruce Palmer
6' 10" Pintail

This clean, mid-1970s 6-foot, 10-inch by 19¾-inch single fin was shaped in the United Kingdom by expatriated Aussie Bruce Palmer. According to Alasdair Lindsay on Vintage Surfboard Collector UK, Bruce started Creamed Honey surfboards in Devon with Kevin Cross and also did a small number of boards under his own label. He was British champ in 1975 and was one of many Aussie surfers who knocked around southwest England in the 1970s, adding much to the quality of UK boards. Palmer also starred in the international surf flick *Playgrounds in Paradise* in 1976 surfing the Severn bore, and the resulting wave was the world's longest ever recorded on film at the time.

Photos by Alex Williams

SURFBOARDS
.. by ..
BRUCE PALMER
Croyde N.Devon

Replica of Shaun Tomson's 1975 Spider Murphy 7' 10" Potato Chip/Banana Board

This is a beautifully crafted replica of the 7-foot, 10-inch Spider Murphy "potato chip" that Shaun Tomson used to shake up the world at the 1975 Pipeline Masters. "Usually design innovation comes about through inspiration. Sometimes it is just a fluke," Shaun said. Spider Murphy made the board for Tomson for Sunset Beach in 1974, which at the time was the site of most pro competitions and was the most important performance big wave in the world.

Photos by Juliana Morais; Board courtesy Fernando Aguerre

Photo by Dan Merkel

Photo by Dan Merkel

The board evolved from a photo of a classic 8-foot Brewer gun that belonged to Jeff Hakman. Murphy worked off that photo and tried to duplicate the rocker, but the molds used in the Safari blanks wouldn't allow it, so he laminated the board and placed bricks on the nose and tried to bend in the rocker. "The board ended up with extreme curve and was an absolute dog on the deep water waves of Sunset, spinning out on turns and very slow," Tomson said.

"However at Pipeline it was a dream, the curve fitting in perfectly to Pipeline's hollow wave face—enabling me to take off later and drive straight off the bottom, and straight off the top." The board was also extremely narrow, and the pintail helped him pull up tight into the tube consistently. Tomson rode that board for five winters at Pipeline and never blew a takeoff—not once. He won the Pipe Masters on that board, and a lot of other Hawaiian contests. "Truly one of the greatest boards of my life. And maybe the first board ever developed with modern rocker that enabled surfers to ride hollow waves differently than they had ever been ridden before."

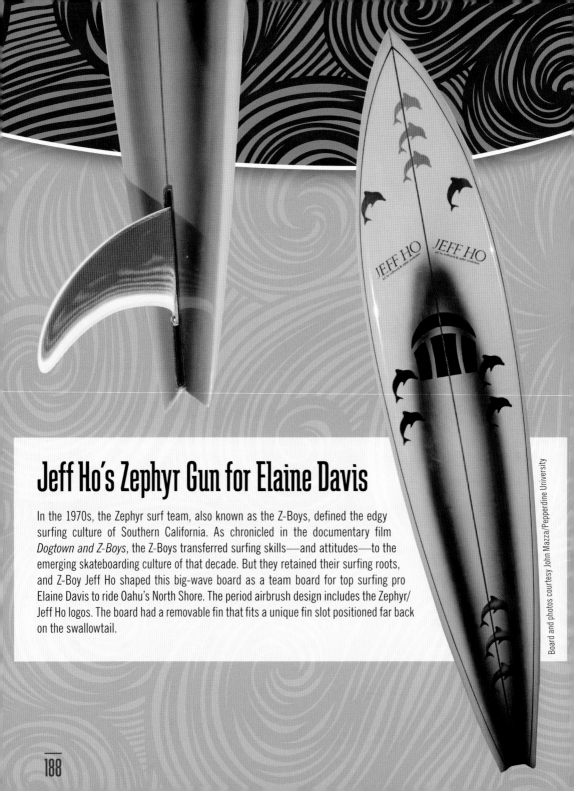

Jeff Ho's Zephyr Gun for Elaine Davis

In the 1970s, the Zephyr surf team, also known as the Z-Boys, defined the edgy surfing culture of Southern California. As chronicled in the documentary film *Dogtown and Z-Boys*, the Z-Boys transferred surfing skills—and attitudes—to the emerging skateboarding culture of that decade. But they retained their surfing roots, and Z-Boy Jeff Ho shaped this big-wave board as a team board for top surfing pro Elaine Davis to ride Oahu's North Shore. The period airbrush design includes the Zephyr/Jeff Ho logos. The board had a removable fin that fits a unique fin slot positioned far back on the swallowtail.

Harold Iggy's
7' 3" SSC Stinger Swallow

This 7-foot, 3-inch Surfboard Shaping Company stinger swallow was shaped by Harold "Iggy" Ige after he ended his employment with Dewey Weber and moved back to Hawaii. Iggy's boards were popular with Bobby Owens and Lynn Boyer. Placed under the feet of Larry Bertlemann, Dane Kealoha, Mark Liddell, and Buttons Kaluhiokalani, the Stinger took small- and medium-sized wave hotdogging to extraordinary levels in the middle of the 1970s. "Anything is possible," Larry Bertlemann declared. But the Stinger's rise was short. By 1977, the twin fin had become the hottest small-wave design.

Photos by Juliana Morais; Board courtesy Fernando Aguerre

Ocean Magic 6' 4" Stinger

The Stinger made it all the way to England by 1977. Ocean Magic shaper Pete "Moony" McAllum apparently reverse-engineered an original Aipa Stinger that 18-year-old Nigel Semmens brought back from England. "This board came from the original Redruth factory before they moved to Newquay," said Alex Williams. "Templates were taken and the design was adapted to British waves. This board came out at 6 feet, 4 inches by 21 inches.

Photo by Lucia Griggi/Lensbaby

Photos by Alex Williams

Allen Sarlo's Wave Killer Board

Allen Sarlo took a lot of heat in the 1970s for his aggressive slashing of waves, when soul styling and flow in black wetsuits on clear surfboards was the go. Dave Gilovich wrote a caption in *Surfing Magazine* along the lines of "Allen Sarlo is the first surfer to kill a wave." That line turned into a nickname—which all accomplished Malibu surfers must have—and in 1977, Bill Urbany shaped this 6-foot by 19¼-inch double-wing swallow with an airbrush by Dana Wolf. Stacy Peralta knows his history, and he argues that the surfing Sarlo was doing in the 1970s was ahead of its time and is now the kind of surfing the world does.

1978 7′ 6″ *Big Wednesday* Lightning Bolt

In 1978, John Milius's answer to *American Graffiti* was *Big Wednesday*, the coming of age story of three surfing friends Matt Johnson (Jan-Michael Vincent), Jack Barlowe (William Katt), and Leroy "The Masochist" Smith (Gary Busey). Toward the end of the movie, Gerry Lopez and his red/yellow Lightning Bolt gun stand as a symbol of changing times. Lopez shows up at Malibu for the biggest day in memory and all eyes are on him, while former surf stars Johnson, Barlowe, and The Masochist are almost forgotten. According to Lopez, this is a replica that he made in Oregon. Randy Rarick sold the original board that Lopez used at Sunset in the final sequence. Jan Michael Vincent's board was sold at an earlier auction for not as much but still a ridiculous amount—for an old surfboard.

Photo by Juliana Morais; Board courtesy Fernando Aguerre

Lord Ted's Lightning Bolt

The UK version of the Lightning Bolt, designed by Viscount Ted Deerhurst—one of the more interesting characters in the surfing world in the second half of the 20th century. Lord Ted was the only son of the 11th Earl of Coventry. More interested in standing up in giant barrels than sitting in the House of Lords, he became Europe's first professional surfer in 1978, joining the new ISP world circuit.

According to Alex Williams, Lord Ted was on Team Bolt and had the rights to make the boards over in the UK. He was having his boards shaped by Tom Parrish, but Tom was also teaching Ted to shape around that time. This board was shaped in Hawaii by Ted, as there is no name on it. Deerhurst later had to change the name of his boards to Excalibur from Sabre in about 1980, due to trademark issues.

Courtesy Steve Daniel

1978 Larry Bertlemann Twin Fin Replica

Santa Cruz Surfboards released this replica of a 1978 Larry Bertlemann twin fin in 2008. The SCS website offers some background on Bertlemann, who is referred to as the "quintessential pioneer of New School surfing. 'Anything is possible' was the mantra he adopted into his mind-bending, space-aged approach to wave riding. Being an avid skateboarder, Bertlemann brought skateboarding to the water. Visualizing street-based maneuvers and adapting them into wave riding was his forte. His skate-influenced wave improvisation was a functional mix of low gravity, high-g cutbacks, 360s, and switch stance surfing. Larry Bertlemann changed the way we ride waves." This Santa Cruz twin fin model epitomizes this blending of the old and the new. The board was designed by Ricky Carroll with graphics by Rasta. The dimensions are 6 feet long by 20 inches wide by 2.6 inches thick. Features include Cruise Missile Concave, single to double vee, a traditional swallowtail, and low entry rocker, and the construction is PowerLyte; this is a molded, sandwich construction surfboard. The board even comes with its own custom-fit, padded board bag—to protect a board that retails for more than $700.

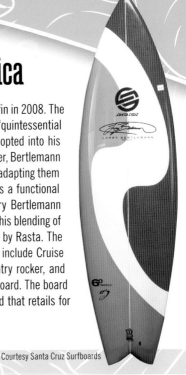

Courtesy Santa Cruz Surfboards

Rolf Aurness's Scaly Hull

It has scales like a fish, but is it a Fish? Malibu restaurateur and raconteur Morgan Runyon explained that this Rolf Aurness hull is 6 feet, 2½ inches long by 18⅝ inches wide. It's a single fin, pre Thruster with two side bite fins. "Kinda Bonzer-like," Runyon said. "Rolf gave me the board in the late '70s early or '80s when we were surfing together."

Aurness is the son of James Arness (different spelling), whom people of a certain age will remember as Marshall Matt Dillon from the TV show *Gunsmoke*. Rolf won the 1970 World Title in Victoria, Australia, at 18 years old, but found he didn't like being a famous surfer and disappeared. Or maybe he just preferred surfing with Morgan Runyon. "I rode the board a bit but was not showing it proper respect," Morgan said. "My neighbor/sister Chenoa Ellis liberated it from me— thus saving it. . . . It's been in storage for a long time with the Ellis family. It's just come back into my life. And I'm waiting for Rolf to show back up for a surf."

Photo and board courtesy Morgan Runyon

Colonel Kilgore's Yater Spoon

This surfboard inspired a song by The Clash. The 9-foot by 21-inch Yater Spoon was the object of Colonel Bill Kilgore's affection in the 1979 movie *Apocalypse Now*. Hollywood has gotten surfers and surfing wrong more than they've gotten it right, but Colonel Kilgore bellowing "Charlie don't surf!" and mounting an air attack on a village just so he could surf Charlie's Point was all very realistic—except for the surfboard. This is not actually a Yater Spoon, and according to Paul Holmes and Chris Dixon of the Honolulu Surfing Museum, "neither of the two boards that appear in the movie are in fact Yater Spoons, but rather nondescript stock longboards that Yater believes were bought off the rack at his Santa Barbara Surf Shop sometime around 1970 and dressed up with artwork by the moviemakers."

One of the boards from the movie is in Francis Ford Coppola's winery in Napa, California. This is the other one.

Board and photos courtesy Jimmy Buffett/Honolulu Surfing Museum

Griff Snyder's 1979 McElhenny Star Bolt

This single fin Star Bolt with the words "McElhenny" on the foam is a personal favorite of collector Griff Snyder. In 1979 he took a trip to Hawaii and walked into the Lightning Bolt shop by the Ala Moana Center. This board was prominently displayed, and it was love at first sight: redwood nose blocks and tail blocks, three stringers, black glue, and a fin to die for. Shaped by Larry McElhenny, this Star Bolt was twice the price of any other board in the shop, but Griff couldn't resist. This board later became his personal first "wall hanger." "I have evacuated my residence several times due to wildfires, and each time this board was one of the first things packed."

Photos by Lucia Griggi; Board courtesy Griff Snyder

1980 Caster Single Fin

The 7-foot, 10-inch Bill Caster is lovely, but seeing as it was made circa 1980, it's kind of
like admiring a dinosaur just before the asteroid hit. Up to 1980, the majority of the surfboards being made and ridden
still had one fin. There were twin fins and Quads and Bonzers and probably other experimental three fins, but the single
fin ruled the world as the decade came to an end.

Photos by Juliana Morais; Board courtesy Fernando Aguerre

Tony Moniz's Reunited 9′ 4″ Aipa Gun

Greg Lui-Kwan is the proud owner of this 9-foot, 4-inch by $19\frac{3}{8}$-inch by 3-inch gun,
which was made by Ben Aipa for Tony Moniz for Waimea. No doubt about it, because
it says so on the foam. "I have so many good memories surfing Waimea alone on
that board," Moniz said. "Early 1980s, that's how it was then. I would call Dane or
someone and say, 'Nobody out Waimea! Let's go paddle!'" Tony used to store all his boards at his mom's place, and at
some point, mom sold this board for $20. When Tony was reunited with his long-lost board in an email, he went all *lolo*.

After hearing the story behind the board, its current owner, Greg Lui-Kwan, spoke to Moniz and told him the board
belongs with him. "I told him about meeting his mom maybe 20 years ago," Lui-Kwan recounted. "I told it full bore with
his mom's speaking style and why she was selling it and what she wanted for it. She was a darling lady. She had a
style. We had a very interesting conversation. Tony got a kick out of the story because his mom died a few years back."

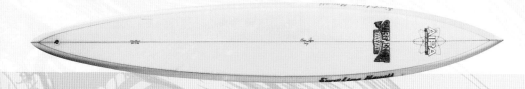

Photos by Greg Lui-Kwan

195

Two Simon Anderson Thrusters

John Mazza's 1981 5-foot, 7-inch Energy Thruster and Fernando Aguerre's 1981 5-foot, 10-inch Energy Thruster are transitional surfboards. The Thruster is one of the most important surfboards in the long evolution. In 1980, Simon Anderson was a pro surfer and a big bloke who was looking for a new "secret weapon." He started with his own version of Australian shaper Geoff McCoy's "no nose" and combined that with a fin setup being used by Australian Frank Williams: a twin fin with a keel-like small single fin at the back. Anderson wanted to make a board that had the speed through the turns of a twin fin but the stability of a single, and the only way to do that was to make a twin fin with a single fin stabilizer at the back.

Anderson morphed three fins onto his "no nose" template and felt that it was good. He reckoned the best way to market his boards was to win pro contests on them. Anderson got a 17th place at the Stubbies contest in Queensland, dominated a 15-foot day at the Bells Beach event, and then beat Cheyne Horan in 3-foot surf. On the Thruster, Simon beat Dane Kealoha and Shaun Tomson in excellent 5-foot Narrabeen. He capped the year by winning the Pipeline Masters on a 7-foot, 6-inch McNabb Thruster.

The Thruster has been the design of choice ever since. "It took a long time and a lot of designing to really bring out the best in the Thruster idea," Nick Carroll wrote. "Basically the thruster stuck a V8 in the Kombi wagon that was the single fin surfboard of 1980. Nobody's out-designed it yet despite countless attempts."

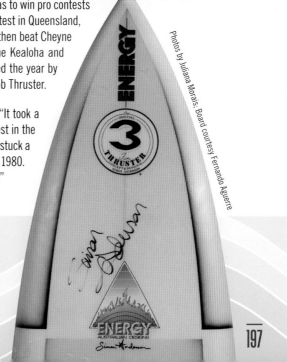

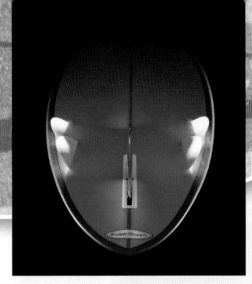

Bonzer Five Fin

The design of the Bonzer Five Fin goes back to 1983, when Australian surfer Glen "Mr. X" Winton was getting results and blowing minds riding a four-fin Quad. The Bonzer brothers figured that single fins and twin fins and Thrusters and Quads were working, so why not go one better. "With all the buzz around the Quads," Malcolm Campbell said in a 2013 interview with LiquidSaltmag.com, "I was thinking maybe there was something we could do with our side fins and make some kind of a hybrid. Around the same time our close friend, Charly Womack, asked me about making him a board with four Bonzer side fins. I told him, 'That's funny Charly, I've been thinking about something like that as well.' . . . We kept the same base length of the three-fin Bonzer side fins, changed the template a bit, divided the fin, and basically moved the front part further out toward the rail. This created a bit of venting between the fins.

"The Bonzer Five will be turning 30 this spring, but it's still looked upon as a relatively new design. I guess that's good for us."

Photos by Chris Park; Board courtesy Bird Huffman

Designed
&
Shaped
by
Jeff Townsley

1982 Circle One Five Fin

This five fin was labeled "a very unique design for the late seventies" by the people at Circle One surfboards in England. This board was shaped by Jeff Townsley for Nigel Whitaker from Clark foam and polyester resin. It was glassed very strong with an 8-ounce glass top and bottom plus an 8-ounce deck patch. Thrusters and Quads had been tested, but this was one of Townsley's first five-fin designs, according to Circle One.

Photos by Alex Williams

Rabbit's 6' 1" Cease and Desist Model

It was a trick to pin an exact year on this 6-foot, 1-inch by 20½-inch Rabbit Bartholomew Hot Stuff channel-bottomed Thruster. Wayne "Mohammed Bugs" Bartholomew thinks that 1983 might be the year it was made. "This may have been one of the last ones made before Warner Brothers made one phone call that was ominous enough to shut the operation down overnight," he recalled.

"When your name comes up at a WB board meeting, you are in hot water. Tom Eberly was making the model in Cal as part of Hot Stuff USA and he fielded the cease and desist phone call. I happened to raise the issue with the Paskowitz family, who said they used to call Mel Blanc 'Uncle Mel.' He, of Bugs Bunny fame, thought the concept quite hilarious but unfortunately he passed away before he could intervene on my behalf." The present owner, Symon Cousens, proudly displays this 1980s icon at Elemental Surf and Skate in Newport, Rhode Island.

Photos by Joe McGovern; Board courtesy Symon Cousens

John Bradbury's 6' 2" Hydrofoil

A mid-1980s board from nose to tail, this 6-foot, 2-inch John Bradbury Hydrofoil was custom-shaped for Fernando Aguerre. Those are first-generation original "Reef Brazil" rice paper logos, first-generation Nose Guard, and Trac-Top traction system with "Secret Weapon" arch bar. Bradbury, a Santa Barbara native, was an early proponent of Styrofoam/epoxy resin boards. According to *The Encyclopedia of Surfing*, he was largely unknown outside of Santa Barbara until 1985, when he made an ultralight Styrofoam/epoxy resin board for future world champion Martin Potter, who immediately rode it to victory in a world pro tour event. Bradbury died of leukemia in 1999 at age 55, likely the result of many years' worth of exposure to toxic board-making materials. Thirty years later, the surfing world has turned to epoxy and other materials that Bradbury was experimenting with in the mid-'80s.

Photo by Juliana Morais; Board courtesy Fernando Aguerre

1980 Schroff Quad

This 5-foot, 9-inch Peter Schroff Baby Swallow four fin is dated 1980. Around the same time Simon Anderson was unleashing the three-fin Thruster on the world, Australian pro Glen "Mr. X" Winton was credited with being one of the surfer/shapers who proved the four-fin Quad as a viable surfboard design. In an interview with Nick Carroll in *Australia's Surfing Life*, Winton admitted that his recipe for the Quad was (Thruster x 2) – twin fin = Quad. "I put six on with the aim of picking one set to knock off," he said. "I actually won a contest on the six. That's how four fins were invented—by knocking two off 'em."

The Quad was and is overshadowed by the Thruster, but the design made it into the 1990s with Will Jobson's Twinzer and Bruce McKee's Quattro. And big-wave shapers like Jeff Clark found the design had advantages in huge waves. More recently, in 2011, Kelly Slater proved the four fin from junk surf at the Quiksilver Pro New York, all the way to winning the 2011 Tahiti Pro in big barrels at Teahupoo, and his spectacular win at the 2013 Volcom Fiji Pro was also on a Quad. Quad is a four-letter word for speed.

Photo by Juliana Morais; Board courtesy Fernando Aguerre

Sandow Birk's *Great War of the Californias*

Painted by Los Angeles artist Sandow Birk, this 7-foot, 6-inch "fun shape" was donated to a Heal the Bay fundraiser in 1990. "The art depicts a study for 'Los Angeles Tea Party' in which Indians throw art made by famous LA artists overboard," said John Mazza. "It is part of a series he did called *The Great War of the Californias*. Birk is a surfer and skateboarder, but most of all he is a well-known artist whose works command very high prices. Of all the boards I own this is the one I probably paid the least for and is now probably one of my most valuable boards."

Photos by Lucia Griggi; Board courtesy John Mazza

Laird Hamilton's Dick Brewer Tow Boards with Heel/Toe Straps

While the New School brethren were shaking up the world of small- to big-wave performance surfing, another school led by Laird Hamilton, Dave Kalama, Buzzy Kerbox, Darrick Doerner, and the Strapped crew was dramatically changing the way men rode mountains. Around 1992, Laird and friends began towing into giant waves using inflatable boats, then jet skis. As the tow surfers began to perfect their art, they realized that the size of a board didn't matter as much in sizeable waves: that is, traditional big-wave guns had too much length and surface area, and the best board for tow surfing was something closer to a water ski. Laird is a strapping 6 feet, 3 inches tall, so these strapped Dick Brewer tow boards are around 7 feet each. The boards are equipped with foot and heel straps, which were an important but overlooked evolution in staying attached to a short, narrow, heavy surfboard going Mach One on a giant wave.

Photo by Sylvain Cazenave

7′ 4″ Skip Frye Swallowtail Painted by Soledad De La Riva

This 7-foot, 4-inch swallowtail was influenced by Bob Simmons and made by Skip Frye for "Fernando of the Reef" for a trip to Costa Rica in 1994. The board was hand painted in 2000 by Argentinian artist Soledad de la Riva, who was inspired by her feelings about the world. "I have gotten some amazing waves on this board in Costa Rica, California, and then Argentina," Fernando said. "The board spent a decade in Argentina as my go-to board for all surfing conditions. Eventually I brought it back to California. . . . It's now displayed in my sweetheart Florencia's office at Greenpacha Hats for a Better World in La Jolla."

Photo by Juliana Morais; Board courtesy Fernando Aguerre

Two from Wingnut's Quiver

Wingnut has a many-faceted personality, and he needs a lot of boards to go with that. Here are two. The board with the red and white stripes is a 9-foot, 4-inch Wingnut model from *Endless Summer 2*. Mike Minchinton shaped 25 of those boards at Robert August Surfboards—and Wingnut made them famous, selling one for $5,000. The board at his feet is a 9-foot, 6-inch Free and Easy by Ernie Tanaka, a heavy vee-bottom single fin with art by D. E. Hardy, pastel chalk on foam.

Which begs a question: What was Wingnut's first surfboard? "My first was a 10-foot Dave Sweet," he said. "It used to be a bar sign—with drink prices on it! I paddled it out at Blackies with a $1.25 Mai Tai still on it!"

Photo by Lucia Griggi

205

Dale Velzy's 12' 2" Swastika Replica

Going back to World War II, Dale Velzy was in the Merchant Marine and went around the world, and that included surfing in Hawaii and Sumatra and a hundred exotic locations. Out of World War II, Velzy was one of the guys who put the "industry" in the "surf industrial complex" as he made boards in the South Bay and opened one of the first surf shops in California. Velzy had financial problems in the 1960s, and he faded with the Shortboard Revolution. But he rose from the ashes in the 1980s with a steady stream of orders for replicas of classic boards from the past. Velzy made this board for surf photographer Leroy Grannis, and it's a tribute to the 1930s, when Pacific Systems Homes hardwood surfboards were "droolers" and out of reach of a kid like Dale Velzy. This board is 12 feet, 2 inches by 22 inches and made of balsa, with seven redwood stringers, a redwood tailblock, and a mahogany fin.

Renny Yater's Big Balsa Bomber

Renny Yater has been mowing balsa going back to the 1950s, and he just can't seem to get enough. This balsa gun is 12 feet, 2 inches by 20¼ inches by 2¾ inches and is dated March 1, 1994, for Jim O'Mahoney at the Santa Barbara Surfing Museum. Within the balsa planks, this gun has five redwood stringers, and it was glassed by Clyde Beatty. "It's hard to find balsa over 12 feet long and I had the wood," O'Mahoney said. "The board's never been surfed, but you could paddle out at Mavericks or Waimea on it tomorrow if you wanted. It's just badass."

Board and photos courtesy Jimmy Buffett/Honolulu Surfing Museum

Magic Sam Flies Again

Nat Young won the 1966 World Contest and changed surfboard history riding a Nat-shaped 9-foot, 4-inch board he called "Magic Sam." That board disappeared and would surely be one of the most valuable surfboards in the world if it turned up. This 9-foot, 4-inch by 22½-inch board is an updated version of Magic Sam. Shaped by Paul Gross for Kirk Putnam, the board was glassed with Volan at Waterman's Guild. According to Putnam, Gross laid out the basic Yater Spoon template on his kitchen floor in Malibu and fine-tuned it for months. "This was many years before everyone had Sam-type boards in their lineup of boards. This one has a fourth gear that will take off without you if you're not ready for it!"

Photo by Kirk Putnam

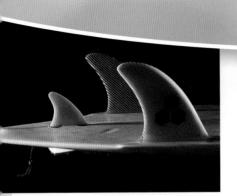

Bird's 1995 Channel Islands MTF

Look close at the foamaglyphics and you'll see this 5-foot, 10-inch by 19½-inch by 2⅝-inch Channel Islands MTF was made personal for Bird Huffman in the mid-2000s. It was shaped by Michael Andrews at Channel Islands. "He nailed it," Bird said, "complete with the fluted wings and all. I had FCS plugs put in it so that traveling was much easier. This board has seen some great Tavarua waves. It is also one that is often borrowed from The Shed. MTF stands for Merrick Twin Finner."

Matt Beard's
Linear Thinking

Matt Beard shaped this *Linear Thinking* board in about 1995, and he rode it heavily for about 10 years. Fast forward to 2008: In an effort to make the artists more integral to a surfboard show, Beard organized a project called the Board Art Benefit. "Board Art started with a dozen artists teaming up with their own shapers and creating unique board art whose sales would benefit SurfAid International," Beard said. "That quickly grew to over 40 boards over the course of 2011–2012. We raised over $30,000 for SurfAid, and the artists were paid nicely as well from the sales that ensued."

Board courtesy Matt Beard

1996 Ogles/Siegfried Camera Board

Before Go Pro revolutionized First Person photography into a 1.6-inch by 2.4-inch by 1.2-inch by 5- to 12-megapixel by 6- to 12-ounce, waterproof package, camera boards were ungainly deals involving big heavy mounts, big heavy cameras, remote controls, and all kinds of gizmos. Back then, surf photographer Ben Siegfried worked with Steve Ogles of Watershot to make rigs. The red board with the rigging was shaped in 1996 by David Craig for Alan Cleland. "The board is 8 feet long," said Siegfried, "but the shape needed to be a bit thicker in the nose for buoyancy to support a 5.5 pound camera/lens/camera-housing. The mount is made from a composite of carbon fiber and fiberglass. This project is significant because it greatly improved on Steve Ogles's camera-board POV from the nose, from his first successful attempts around 1974."

1996 Tandem Board with Camera Mount

The tandem board was shaped by Hobie Surfboards in 1996 for Brian and Illa McEvilly, a tandem surfing pair. The board is 12 feet long and has custom board artwork executed by George Gall, art directed by Ben Siegfried. The mount was the same as the red board, but with the obvious benefit of size, the tandem was the most stable glide in the fleet.

Courtesy Ben Siegfried and Steve Ogles

Steve Ogles's Yellow Rusty and iPhone Housings

Exclusively for this book, Steve Ogles dared to bring a surfboard encrusted with wax and sand into his spotless, macrobiotic, bird-friendly, Free Trade, clean room/workshop in Coronado, California. The board is Steve's. "The board in the portrait is an ARC Tail, or by more recent vernacular, a reverse Tubercle Tail. . . . Rick Hamon shaped all of them. I had been riding Fish and wanted something short with a spruce stringer, a split tail, and 3 fins, but something truly my own with a nice big curve. I like small waves, small boards, 3 fins, light winds, sunshine, and curves. The board in the image is my 5th or 6th Arc Tail, all shaped by Rick."

In front of Steve, also in yellow, is the state of the art in waterproof cell phone housings. Steve is a captain for American Airlines flying 737s. Watershot is his side-job, but he got out of camera housings for surfboards while the getting was good and moved into making beautiful, high-tech camera housings for Hollywood. *Pirates of the Caribbean* and a whole bunch of other movies shot their water sequences using Zuccarini Watershot housings.

Watershot also makes a line of camera housings for the iPhone 4/4S and iPhone 5, which can be mounted on a surfboard and reduces that 5.5 pound housing/camera combination to about 6¼ inches by 3¾ inches by 1⅜ inches and weighing from 17 ounces to 19.5 ounces, depending on the model and lens selection.

Norrin Radd's Inter-Galactic Plank

Of course you know the Silver Surfer was born Norrin Radd on the planet Zenn-La and that he made a deal with the devil Galactus the World Devourer to become his herald and seek out new worlds if Galactus would spare Zenn-La. And that Galactus transformed Norrin Radd into a silver-skinned, cosmic-powered super-being who zooms around the universe on a cosmic board that resembles a surfboard.

But did you know Silver Surfer's board was made of unknown materials and is laminated with a silvery glaze that make the surfboard impervious to all forms of physical damage, short of the cosmic power of Galactus?

According to Paul Holmes and Chris Dixon, Jim O'Mahoney knew all that and contacted Silver Surfer creator Stan Lee for permission to re-create the Silver Surfer's plank using earthly materials. Stan Lee directed O'Mahoney to Marvel Comics, and after a year of wrangling, they granted him permission to make exactly one board that followed the design laid out in the comic book. The 9-foot by 18-inch board with the distinctive five lines on the deck was made of T-6061 aircraft aluminum by master metal fabricator Henry Weir, a renowned hot rod mechanic. The board weighs 97 pounds, so the core must be Kryptonite or Plutonium or whatever.

When it was done, Stan Lee saw that it was good and signed a letter stating: "I, the co-creator, deem Norrin Radd, also known as the Silver Surfer, the only one to use this board in his quests both on earth and throughout the universe."

MVP Books collection

Crazy Connie's Masterpiece

John Whitmer of Oregon by way of Florida sent in this 7-foot, 10-inch board painted from nose to tail by a woman he called "Crazy Connie"—a Bedouin lady who lived in Whitmer's part of Florida and a fairly good surfer. She wanted a "fun gun" for bigger surf, and Whitmer shaped her a board in the Rusty Desert Island mold. "After I shaped the board she asked if she could paint it," Whitmer recalled. "I was very leery and scolded her on how vulnerable unshaped blanks are, no possibility of erasure or correction, etc."

Crazy Connie disappeared with the board for months, and Whitmer forgot all about it. Nine months later she showed up with the board painted with every type of ocean life from reef to birds. The deck is ringed with Bible verses relating to the sea. "I was amazed at the detail and the amount of work she had done," Whitmer said. "Also even more amazed when she said she had never really done any painting until this board." He glassed the board with trepidation, but it came out great. Connie kept the board at his shop and rode it occasionally. When Whitmer was moving to Oregon, he bought the board. "She had the idea it was worth several thousand dollars. I said maybe to an art collector or something but not in the real world. I gave her $500 cash, which I hoped would get her back on her feet."

Donny Wright's 10-Foot Bore Rider

David Macdonald Damerell Morshead Macer-Wright has a name almost as long as those tidal bore waves he likes to surf. The producer and director of the 2005 documentary *Longwave*, Donny Wright (for short) stood with a 10-foot-long by 23¾-inch-wide by 2¾-inch-thick longboard designed for surfing both the Severn tidal bore and regular ocean waves. "This board is the result of my friendship with Guts Griffiths, who became European Longboard Champion the year he shaped the board for me," said Wright. "In the late '90s it was unique in the UK surf breaks for its size and weight. I used to get some funny looks but also with time a lot of friendly vibe for style in the water. . . . It's not the fastest of boards and I reckon that's why it handles so well in big, fat waves. I've surfed it solo in double overhead surf at Brandon Bay, west coast Ireland."

Courtesy Donny Wright

John Holm's
8′ 4″ Donald Takayama Tribute

John Holm's 8-foot, 4-inch by 22⅛-inch by 3⅛-inch Donald Takayama Hawaiian Pro Designs Egg goes back to a time when the Seattle artist was living in Los Angeles. When he was enrolled at the LA Art Center he would go to Malibu every weekend to surf. Around 1998 Holm was working on a commercial in Los Angeles and wanted to surf Malibu again. He was 52 and a little out of shape but went to Malibu and bought this board, walked across Pacific Coast Highway and surfed. The board is a tri fin with the outside fins glassed in. Holm wasn't sure what year the board was shaped, but he did the art in 2013. "I have enjoyed the Egg on surfing trips with my kids here in the Northwest," Holm said. "Of course it has special meaning now since Donald has passed." Takayama died of a heart attack in October of 2012.

Courtesy John Holm

Photo by Lucia Griggi

Gary Linden's 9' 0" Balsa Gun

The founder of the Big Wave World Tour, Gary Linden knows that size matters: He likes paddling into big waves, likes looking at them, likes being around them. They energize his life. Linden also loves making boards for big waves out of whatever material you like—agave, balsa, sometimes even foam and fiberglass. "This is a balsa Todos Santos gun with a larger middle fin and two side bites," Linden said. "A period piece shaped in the late nineties." This board caught the attention of Fernando Aguerre at a trade show, and the shaper and the collector made a deal. It was on display at the original Reef headquarters for many years and was the model that Skip Staats rode at Killer's for many years.

Photo by Juliana Morais; Board courtesy Fernando Aguerre

Gary Linden's
10' 4" Simmons Replica in Agave

Agave is a succulent plant that grows in the desert. Distill agave sap, and you have mescal tequila. Agave is a food source, the fibers can be made into rope, and the stalks, when hollowed out, make passable didgeridoo. A clever plant used by a clever species. Gary Linden is also native to a desert land, and he uses agave to make surfboards. This is a replica of a Bob Simmons board from another era. Linden made the Simmons replica as a joint project with Dr. Mark Bracker, who made the agave blank. The board is 10 feet, 4 inches by 24 inches by 3½ inches and extremely light for its size. Linden used an original Simmons that belonged to Bird Huffman as a reference. "It really took me back in time as I attempted to duplicate the curves, imagining how they would function," Linden said. "Fernando [Aguerre] saw it at a trade show and immediately had to have it. I made him swear he would surf it and he did many times, telling me later how much fun it was to ride."

Photos by Juliana Morais; Board courtesy Fernando Aguerre

9' 6" Todos Santos Agave Gun

This is an agave Todos Santos model gun that was made by Gary Linden for Fernando Aguerre's collection in the early 2000s. The board measures 9 feet, 6 inches by 19½ inches by 3 inches. "As time went by," Linden said, "the guns became thicker and wider, and this one is the end of the sleeker-style gun."

Agave 6' 8" Swallowtail by Gary Linden

Gary Linden loves agave but doesn't only make big-wave guns with the material. This is an agave 6-foot, 8-inch Fish shaped for Fernando Aguerre, but it turned out to be too "modern" for what he was looking for. It was treated with a wood stain to give it an older look, the only one Linden ever did with this method.

Guilhem's Grenouille

Great Britain is well represented in this book, but what about their brother surfers on the other side of the English Channel? France has really good surf and some really good surfers, and they are an arty, fashionable bunch, so you have to figure they make lovely surfboards as well. Guilhem Rainfray describes himself as the "owner, shaper, glasser, sander, glosser, polisher, and floor-sweeper at Guéthary Surfboards, Guéthary, France." And he has been refining these skills going back to 1969. This is the 9-foot, 6-inch by 23-inch by 3-inch longboard Guilhem made in 2009 for his friend Stéphane Garnier's 40th birthday. It's a basic, old-style longboard with 50/50 rails. Guilhem carved a "Just Foam" 9-foot, 8-inch blank with a 1-inch balsa T-band and 2-inch by ⅛-inch red cedar sides. He routed the "Figure 8" stringers and fitted them in the blank. Translucent resin nose and tail blocks, which he also made, had small pearl hearts and a faux sapphire embedded. The fiberglass leash loop has the number "40" carved in it.

Photo by Sebastien Marie; Board courtesy Guilhem Rainfray

Modern Brewer Balsa Gun

Twelve-foot balsa guns are rare because most balsa planks come no longer than 10 feet. But Dick Brewer apparently loves mowing balsa, because he made this 12-footer, now in the collection of Fernando Aguerre, in 2000.

Photos by Juliana Morais; Board courtesy Fernando Aguerre

Gerry Lopez's Personal 7′ 4″ Tow Board

Gerry Lopez shaped this 7-foot, 4-inch tow board for himself in 2000 and surfed it many a time at Jaws. It's finished in classic Lopez colors. When asked for additional info, Gerry said: "That about covers it. Got the Chiemsee Plus/Minus logo. Notice the heavy t-band stringer. . . . It was some special, ultra-high-density Clark Foam that Grubby Clark blew especially for us for tow boards." The stringer is ½-inch basswood, ⅛-inch red cedar, ½-inch basswood, and the board was glassed with polyester resin and multiple layers of fiberglass.

Photo by Juliana Morais; Board courtesy Fernando Aguerre

Andy Irons's Carper Retro Rocket

At the second Doris Duke Surf Fest on July 14, 2012, Brian Sargent of Newport, Rhode Island, stands with a Retro Rocket shaped by John Carper for Andy Irons. Written on the foam is the board's specs: 6 feet, 3 inches by 18.65 inches by 2.25 inches. Sargent holds in his hand an image from Woodshed Films' *One Track Mind*, but even with high-resolution digital photography, it's impossible to verify if the board in his hand is the same as the board in his other hand.

Photo by Joe McGovern

2001 White Lightning's 7′ 10″ Hawaiian Gun

This 7-foot, 10-inch Hawaiian gun for Mick Fanning dates from the year he began to let the world know what White Lightning was all about. The New School had a good run through most of the 1990s, but by Y2K there was a Newer School of pro surfers challenging Kelly Slater, Taylor Knox, Rob Machado, and their band of merry men. One of them was Mick Fanning, a determined Queenslander and one of three "Coolie Kids"—along with Joel Parkinson and Dean Morrison—who began to shake up the world of pro surfing around the turn of the century. In 2001 Fanning won the Rip Curl Pro Bells Beach as a wildcard, and that gave the world a heads up to what was coming: the World Title in 2007 and 2009 and gunning for a third in 2013. This board was shaped October 23, 2001, according to writing on the foam, which you can see under the paint job and all the stickers.

Photos by Juliana Morais; Board courtesy Fernando Aguerre

6′ 5″ Mentawai Memento

During Fernando Aguerre's first trip to the Mentawai Islands in 2001, his good friend Cesar Colombo (several times Argentinean surfing champion) bought this 6-foot, 5-inch board from a local surfer as a thank you present for Fernando. Crafted by an unknown shaper, the board is made of a local wood and features several folk art designs seen in other wooden artifacts in the Islands. It's a one-of-a-kind board with a very proper outline, boat-type rocker in both nose and tails, but very thin.

Photos by Juliana Morais; Board courtesy Fernando Aguerre

Evocative Andy Irons and Kelly Slater Surfboards

This photo of Andy Irons's 6-foot, 4-inch Arakawa towering over Kelly Slater's 6-foot Channel Islands says a lot about their relationship in the first five years of the 21st century. Slater won six out of seven world titles from 1992 to 1998 and then didn't compete from 1999 to 2001 while Irons began his rise. The leader of the New School, Slater was starting to feel like old school, and that didn't sit well with a chap who is about as competitive as the entire nation of China. Beginning in 2002, Slater was back on tour where he and Irons engaged in epic battles. Slater finished ninth in 2002, while Irons took the world title. Slater finished second in 2003, while Irons took the world title. Irons won the world title again in 2004 while Slater took third. And then in 2005, Slater won his seventh world title with Irons finishing second. These two boards represent that period from 2001 to 2005, when Andy Irons towered over Kelly Slater and their rivalry rocked the surfing world.

Photo by Chris Park; Boards courtesy Bird's Surf Shed

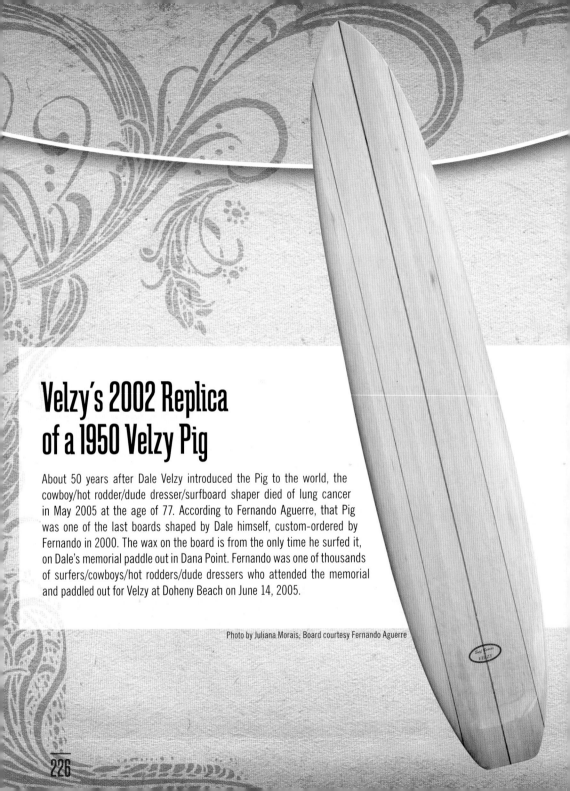

Velzy's 2002 Replica of a 1950 Velzy Pig

About 50 years after Dale Velzy introduced the Pig to the world, the cowboy/hot rodder/dude dresser/surfboard shaper died of lung cancer in May 2005 at the age of 77. According to Fernando Aguerre, that Pig was one of the last boards shaped by Dale himself, custom-ordered by Fernando in 2000. The wax on the board is from the only time he surfed it, on Dale's memorial paddle out in Dana Point. Fernando was one of thousands of surfers/cowboys/hot rodders/dude dressers who attended the memorial and paddled out for Velzy at Doheny Beach on June 14, 2005.

Photo by Juliana Morais; Board courtesy Fernando Aguerre

HANG IT.
RIP IT.
SHRED IT.
RIDE IT.

BLUE CRUSH

Photo by Lucia Griggi; Boards courtesy John Mazza

Boards by Eden Props from *Blue Crush*

The Eden label looks familiar, but it's all just a fantasy. These are two boards used in the movie *Blue Crush*, a 2002 Brian Grazer/ John Stockwell production that grossed $40 million and inspired a spike in the number of women in the water. John Mazza bought the boards from a prop house with a certificate of authenticity. "There were three copies made of each board," Mazza said. "The yellow board was used by Anne Marie [Kate Bosworth] and the red board was used by Eden [Michelle Rodriguez]. Both boards appear on the poster." A trained foamaglyphics expert looked at these boards and saw the little fish symbol, which told him: "John Carper." These are both Carper Rocket Guns. The red board is 6 feet 6 inches by 18 inches by 2.15 inches, and the yellow board is 6 feet, 3 inches by 17.4 inches by 2 inches.

Drew Brophy's Rolling Stones Tribute

Surfers love to fly off the lip, but they also love flying lips. Drew Brophy painted this tropically toothy tribute to Mick and Keith in 2003, on a 9-foot, 6-inch double wing pin shaped by Ron House. But the surfer fascination with the Rolling Stones goes way back, at least as far as 1982 and the movie *Fast Times at Ridgemont High*.

Jeff Spicoli: Where'd you get this jacket?
Stu Nahan: I got this from the network. Let me ask you a question. What's next for Jeff Spicoli?
Jeff Spicoli: Heading over to the Australian and Hawaiian internationals, and then me and Mick are going to wing on over to London and jam with the Stones!

This board is on display at the Hard Rock Casino.

Board courtesy Drew Brophy

Drew Brophy's *Voodoo Child*

The surfer fascination with Jimi Hendrix goes back at least as far as the 1972 movie *Rainbow Bridge*, which included a small Hendrix concert on Maui with surfing by David Nuuhiwa and friends. But the fascination went both ways, as near the end of Hendrix's 1967 song "Third Stone from the Sun," Hendrix cryptically says: "And you'll never hear surf music again." Those words have been analyzed ever since. Some people think Hendrix didn't like surf music and knew that the British Invasion of the late 1960s was going to end the genre. Dick Dale says that he was stricken with cancer at the time and was rumored to be dying. Hendrix played guitar left-handed like Dale and considered the pioneering surf guitarist an inspiration: "You'll never hear surf music again" was a tribute to Dale.

Drew Brophy painted *Voodoo Child* on a Ron House 9-foot, 6-inch double wing gun and it's been on permanent display at the Hard Rock Casino in Las Vegas since 2000.

Sli Dawg's
5' 8" Hendrix Tribute

What we have here on the bottom of this 5-foot, 8-inch Fish is another Jimi Hendrix tribute, painted by artist Sli Dawg for former pro surfer and Billabong exec Paul Naude. This board can be found in Fernando Aguerre's house—and in the seminal surfboard history book, *The Surfboard: Art, Style, Stoke*.

Photo by Juliana Morais; Board courtesy Fernando Aguerre

Mike Diffenderfer 9′ 10″ Balsa

Mike Diffenderfer shaped his first balsa board in 1951, and he estimates he shaped between 20,000 to 25,000 boards in his lifetime. This is one of the last three he shaped before he passed on in 2002. This 9-foot, 10-inch board is made of balsa with redwood stringers and rails.

Photos by Juliana Morais; Board courtesy Fernando Aguerre

2003 Andy Irons
6′ 2″ Channel Islands

That DC sticker close to the tail covers up the foamaglyphics on this Channel Islands 6-foot, 2-inch board, but the writing on the nose says a bit. This board belonged to Andy Irons and was most likely one of his competition boards during the 2003 season. According to Graham Stapelberg, a former ASP exec who worked with Andy for many years at Billabong, "Andy would get boards from quite a few different shapers. In the USA he mainly used Mayhem and CI boards. In the beginning he used Eric Arakawa (HIC) boards."

Photo by Juliana Morais; Board courtesy Fernando Aguerre

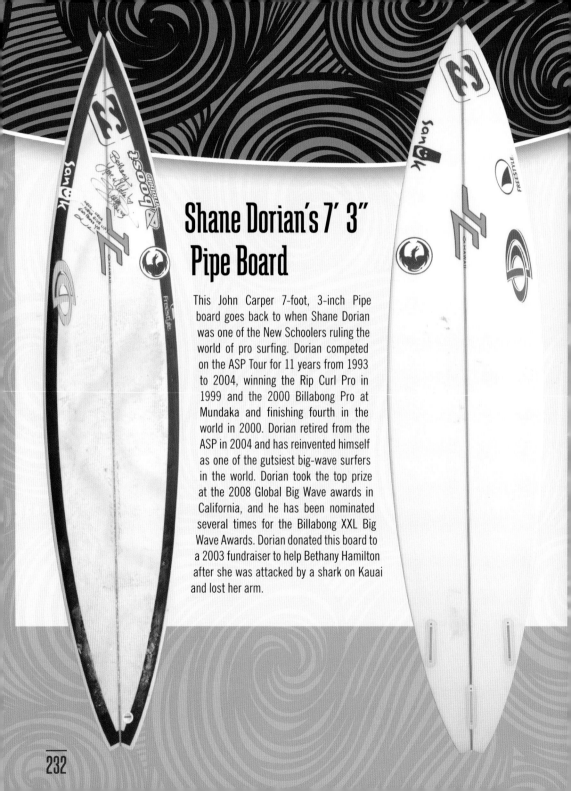

Shane Dorian's 7' 3" Pipe Board

This John Carper 7-foot, 3-inch Pipe board goes back to when Shane Dorian was one of the New Schoolers ruling the world of pro surfing. Dorian competed on the ASP Tour for 11 years from 1993 to 2004, winning the Rip Curl Pro in 1999 and the 2000 Billabong Pro at Mundaka and finishing fourth in the world in 2000. Dorian retired from the ASP in 2004 and has reinvented himself as one of the gutsiest big-wave surfers in the world. Dorian took the top prize at the 2008 Global Big Wave awards in California, and he has been nominated several times for the Billabong XXL Big Wave Awards. Dorian donated this board to a 2003 fundraiser to help Bethany Hamilton after she was attacked by a shark on Kauai and lost her arm.

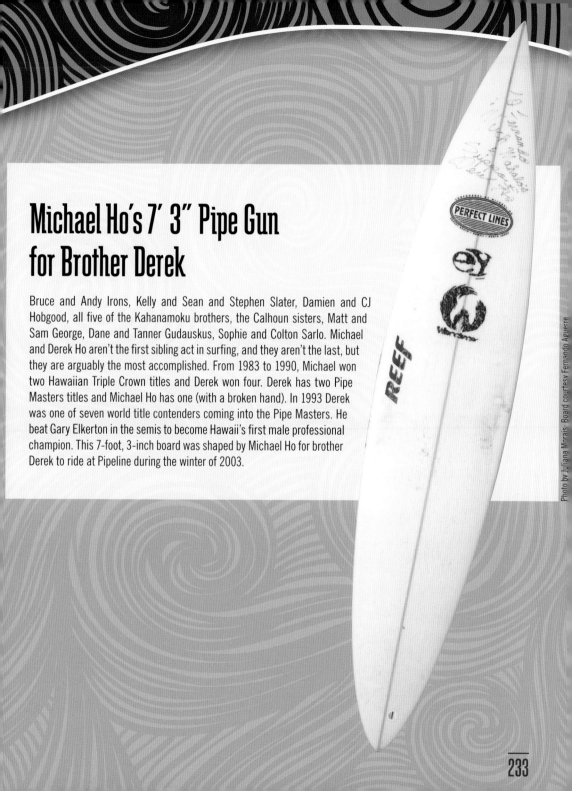

Michael Ho's 7' 3" Pipe Gun for Brother Derek

Bruce and Andy Irons, Kelly and Sean and Stephen Slater, Damien and CJ Hobgood, all five of the Kahanamoku brothers, the Calhoun sisters, Matt and Sam George, Dane and Tanner Gudauskus, Sophie and Colton Sarlo. Michael and Derek Ho aren't the first sibling act in surfing, and they aren't the last, but they are arguably the most accomplished. From 1983 to 1990, Michael won two Hawaiian Triple Crown titles and Derek won four. Derek has two Pipe Masters titles and Michael Ho has one (with a broken hand). In 1993 Derek was one of seven world title contenders coming into the Pipe Masters. He beat Gary Elkerton in the semis to become Hawaii's first male professional champion. This 7-foot, 3-inch board was shaped by Michael Ho for brother Derek to ride at Pipeline during the winter of 2003.

Photo by Juliana Morais; Board courtesy Fernando Aguerre

233

2003 Joe Quigg Complete Combination Replica

Joe Quigg hand-shaped this 9-foot, 10-inch replica of the famous Darrylin Zanuck board in 2003 from a chambered balsa blank. This is the same design that Quigg shaped in 1947 for surfing big Rincon in California. The shape was way ahead of its time, featuring the same 50/50 rails, pintail, and progressive rocker used in today's boards. Quigg calls it the "complete combination," his single most important contribution to the surfing world. The original board—then tested by Dave Rochlen, Tommy Zahn, and Pete Peterson—was instantly judged as a breakthrough in shaping design. Along with Bob Simmons and Matt Kivlin, Quigg is justly considered one of the fathers of the modern surfboard.

Kelly Slater's 7' 2" Jedi Gun

This 7-foot, 2-inch Channel Islands gun is the kind of board Kelly Slater rides to shock and awe the world in Hawaii. "He can see things before they happen. That's why he appears to have such quick reflexes. It's a Jedi trait." That was Qui-Gon Jin's appraisal of young Anakin Skywalker, but anyone who has seen Kelly Slater surfing in Hawaii wonders if he has some Jedi blood. When Kelly Slater spins around and takes off super late at Backdoor, as he is skittering into the barrel, he sets a line that seems to know what that end section is going to do—before that end section exists. Kelly is blessed with remarkably obedient, fast-twitch muscle fibers all connected to his experienced Gulliver. But fast reflexes aren't worth much without an obedient surfboard like this 7-foot, 2-inch Merrick under his feet.

Photos by Juliana Morais; Board courtesy Fernando Aguerre

Rob Machado's 8-Foot Channel Islands Gun

Since its founding in 1984, Reef Brazil has sponsored a lot of great surfers: helping them travel around the world and tune their quivers and their bodies, pay mortgages, and raise families. Rob Machado first signed with Reef Brazil in the 1990s, and in 2012, he signed a deal that would keep him on Team Reef until 2015.

In 2003, Machado showed his gratitude to Reef founder Fernando Aguerre by signing this 8-foot Channel Islands gun. Machado left no doubt as to its function in how he signed the board: "To Fernando. You can only ride this board at the Banzai Pipeline. Happy surfing and thanks for everything."

Photos by Juliana Morais; Board courtesy Fernando Aguerre

Rochelle Ballard's
6′ 1″ Channel Islands

Asked about this 6-foot, 1-inch Channel Islands board from circa 2003, Rochelle Ballard said that she rode it at Cloud Break in Fiji and in Tahiti. "It was some of my best memories being on tour," she said, "surfing Teahupoo and staying in a little boat house next to the boat launch in the same place that Andy Irons and Kai Borg always stayed. The mommy and pappy fixed up the little boat house for me and my good friend Sky to stay in. No one wanted to stay in it because it had rats in the roof. Mommy cleaned it up, got the rats out and made it so cute with Tahitian floral design. That year, riding that 6-foot, 1-inch, I remember the waves being really nice. Clean 4 to 8 feet. Sweet barrels, fresh sashimi, Hinanos, and epic company."

Photos by Juliana Morais; Board courtesy Fernando Aguerre

2003 Taylor Knox Channel Islands 6′ 2″

Taylor Knox signed this 6-foot, 2-inch Channel Islands board over to Fernando Aguerre in 2003, the year Knox finished seventh on the World Tour. This came 10 years after Knox's first full season on the ASP Tour, and in that 10 years, Knox finished as high as 4th (2001) and as far back as 35th (1998). A graph of his competitive career would look like the flight of a drugged-out bumblebee.

Knox has a long relationship with Al Merrick, developing boards like the Fort Knox, which he rode all the way to the bank in 2009 and 2010, and the Dagger, made in 2013 and based on a Tom Curren outline. Ten years later, Knox wasn't on the 2013 WCT Tour for only the second time in 20 years. That's an impressive record for a guy who has overcome serious injuries over the years. He'll be back.

Dale Webster's
10,407-Days Longboard

In front of the spooky school house used by Hitchcock in *The Birds*, Dale Webster stands with his 9-foot, 7-inch five-fin longboard made by Bonzer Brother Malcolm Campbell. Shaped in 2002, the 10,407 written in wax on the board refers to—get this—the total number of consecutive days Dale Webster went surfing, from 1975 to 2004. "The most important date for the board," Webster said, "was, is, and always will be Sunday, February 29th. This was a Leap Year day in 2004, and it came exactly 28 years since the last time Leap Year day fell on a Sunday, in 1976. (I missed a day in 1975)."

Webster didn't quit after Leap Year day 2004. "That board was retired and replaced with a replica," he said. "I retired after 13,000 days with another replica of the first, but I forgot to strap it on my car and dinged it. I'm surfing the original again with a decade-old wax job."

So Dale Webster surfed every day, without fail from the Ford presidency to the Obama presidency and not only that, he did it in the vicinity of Bodega Bay: a sharky, cold, windy, stormy, unforgiving, lonely place that can be summed up in a word: spooky.

Photos by Lucia Griggi/Lensbaby

Peruvian Pride

Sofia Mulanovich was a girl from nowhere in Peru who overcame the tyrannies of distance, poverty, language, and other tyrannies to win three out of six World Championship Tour events and claim the 2004 World Title. Sofia was the first South American to claim a professional surfing world title. Sofia had help along the way from Reef and others, and in 2004 she signed this board to Fernando Aguerre: "For Fernando. Muchas gracias por el apoyo! Aqui te doy una tabla que me ayudo mucho. Con carino. Sofia Mulanovich." Running that through Google Translate we get: "Thank you very much for your support! Here I give you a table that helped me a lot. With affection." Well actually *tabla* can also mean "surfboard," and this 5-foot, 7-inch Merrick is an M4 model.

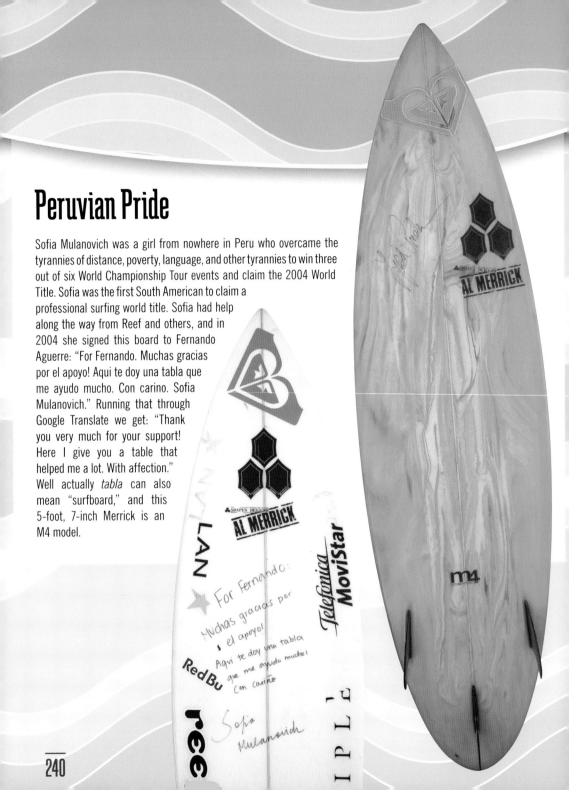

Joe Curren's 6' 4" MBM Model

Son of Pat Curren and brother of Tom Curren, Joe Curren inherited more than a little bit of that surfing DNA. A hyperactive kid, Joe started surfing during the El Nino winter of 1983 on a 5-foot, 9-inch Merrick hand-me-down from Tom, who broke the board at Sandspit. Joe's second board was custom made by Tom. Two decades and dozens of boards later, Joe was riding this 6-foot, 4-inch Al Merrick. According to Joe, "I can only tell it's mine by the Seven Two sticker [part of OP] who sponsored me in 2003–2004. It was probably an MBM model [Bobby Martinez model]."

Marc Andreini's Quartet of Gliders

Marc Andreini was raised on longboards and loves the flow and glide from that era but not the performance. He shaped this collection of "personal gliders" for himself between 1991 and 2012, developed for Northern California where he rides lots of open-water, large surf–style breaks. The boards have more rocker and deep hull and vee to handle high speed winter power. The glider combines the best of the 1960s and the transition to performance. "The Camo was made in 2005," Andreini said. "It is number six of my personal 11-foot gliders. I made the first one in 1991, inspired by Skip Frye, who was inspired by the Duke on his 16-footer at Waikiki. . . . I use the 12-footer [right] at Cowells on smaller days, although I still sneak a few at Center Peak through Cowells!"

Photo courtesy Marc Andreini

Bella Bellisima

From the hands of Marc Andreini this 9-foot, 1-inch by 21¼-inch by 3.35-inch by 26 pound "Bella" was featured under his bare, freezing feet at Jeffrey's Bay in the 2005 movie *Chasing Dora*. This movie followed three surfers who followed guidelines for a contest laid down by Miki Dora in the article "Aquatic Ape" published in a 2002 issue of *The Surfer's Journal*. Contestants had to make a board no bigger than 9 feet 6 inches and no smaller than 8 feet with a tail block no smaller than 10 inches. Single fin, no plastics, no logos. With no leash, contestants would ride their boards on an 8-foot to 10-foot day at Jeffrey's Bay with no wetsuit. The winner would be he who got the longest ride. "This board was made and surfed by me for the film," Andreini said. "I shaped 'Bella' in 2005 with balsa redwood and wood glue with a varnish finish. This is the most meaningful board I ever made."

Megan Halavais's Shark-Bit Board

This is the modern shortboard that 20-year-old Megan Halavais was paddling at Salmon Creek in northern California in October of 2005 when she was attacked by a great white shark. A marine biologist measured the imprint of the shark bite and estimated the shark to be 20 feet long and weighing 2,000 pounds. Halavais was injured and flown to the hospital but made a full recovery—although without insurance, her medical expenses were as savage as the shark. The money she got from this board helped to pay for some of her medical expenses.

Renny Yater and Kevin Ancell's *The Ark*

A masterpiece carved on a masterpiece, this 11-foot, 4-inch by 17½-inch Yater "stiletto gun" was scrimshawed by the intricate and omnipotent hand of artist Kevin Ancell. Known for his angry, animatronic *Aloha Ao* hula girls with machine guns, Ancell is the artist behind some of the most beautiful surfboards ever made, especially those inlaid with abalone shell.

Renny Yater and Ancell met at the Santa Monica art gallery Track 16 and began a collaboration to push the boundaries of the "art board" market. This board was shaped from a balsa wood blank by Yater in late 2007. The artwork tableau is a quirky, illustrated timeline history of surfing from ancient times in Hawaii to contemporary tow-in, big-wave riding where a surfer speeds from the impending grasp of God's hand. For someone like Ancell, who grew up being inspired by the Santa Monica-Venice surf and art milieu that fomented fine artists like Robert Irwin and Billy Al Bengston and the surf and skate art of Z-Boys and Santa Monica Airlines, the Yater connection is the fulfillment of a natural progression of interests and ideas. "The cool thing is he's a pretty conservative old-world California type and I'm a complete maniac," explained Ancell. "So he keeps me from doing stuff that's completely nuts and makes sure we get a clean look." For Yater, it is equally rewarding. "We're just having fun combining our talents, combining the old and the new," says the master shaper.

Board and photos courtesy Jimmy Buffett/Honolulu Surfing Museum

Entertainment Center

There is a lot of sitting and waiting in surfing; the waves don't pump through all the time. This 5-foot, 10-inch Spyder five fin is equipped with a Go Pro for taking action shots or practicing your Shakespeare soliloquies, and it also has a slot for an iPhone that attaches to waterproof speakers. So you can rock out to tunes as you're sitting and as you're riding. Just don't listen to the theme from *Jaws*.

Alex Kopps's Shot-Up Fish

Alex Kopps painted this Al Merrick Fish in 2005 for the Surfrider Foundation's Art for the Oceans, a surfboard art auction to raise money to support Surfrider's quest to protect oceans, waves, and beaches. Steve Blank is the director of development for the Surfrider Foundation, and he had the 411 on this board: "This one by Kopps is interesting because a) he was the only guy who waxed his board and surfed it and b) he painted a pink bull's-eye on the bottom and then shot the board repeatedly with a BB gun. The Polaroid attached to the board depicts his time on the firing range."

Boards courtesy Alex Kopps and the Surfrider Foundation

247

Moondoggie's Benefit Board

Billy Al Bengston was a Golden Age surfer and member of the Malibu Pit crew while attending Los Angeles City College (1952), California College of Arts & Crafts (1955), and the Otis Art Institute (1956). His nickname "Moondoggie" was usurped by the movie *Gidget*. Bengston's first solo show was at the Ferus Gallery in 1958, and through the 1960s, he evolved into one of the most influential artists on the West Coast. This is the board Bengston painted for the Surfrider Foundation's 2005 Art for the Oceans benefit. He used sign-writer enamel to paint both sides of the board.

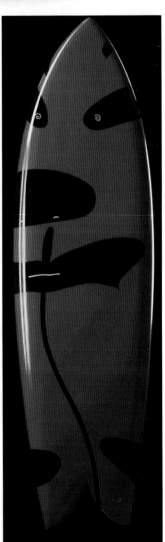

Colleen Hanley's Billabong Board

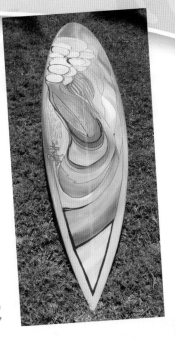

Colleen Hanley is an artist who surfs or a surfer who creates imagery designed primarily from experiences as a surfer—on canvas, wood, surfboards, and fabric. Hanley painted this in 2005 on a 9-foot Timmy Patterson gun. It was one of five boards chosen for display permanently in Billabong's Times Square store, their first retail location. "I used a paint brush for all the colors," Hanley said. "And a black ink marker Posca pen for outline."

This board holds a special place in Hanley's early art career as it was her first big commission deal for a client she had respected for a long time. Hanley's board was part of the display in Billabong's New York store. "My parents are from the Bronx, so I just felt like I conquered a little something for my inner self as a female surf artist."

Dave Hobrecht's Curren Tribute

Laguna Beach artist Dave Hobrecht paints all kinds of athletes, from Babe Ruth to thoroughbred horses—and that includes surfers. Hobrecht grew up admiring the smooth surfing of Tom Curren, and when it came to time paint a board for the Art for the Oceans Benefit, "instead of painting Tom in the water I painted him out of the ocean, playing music—his other passion. That's why it's called *Style In and Out*. The board is now owned by Lance Anderson."

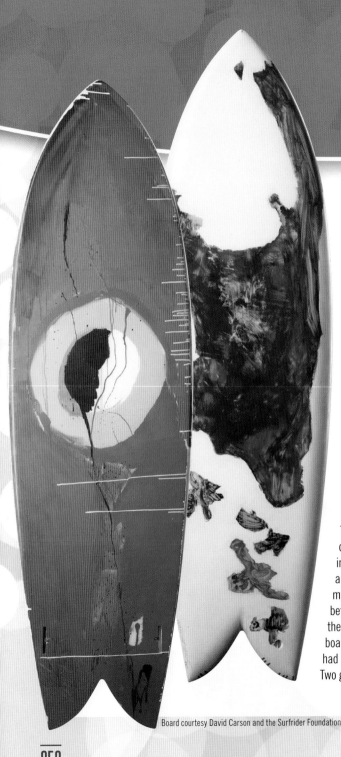

David, Luke, and Luci's Thick Fish

This Fish was delivered by FedEx to David Carson's home in the British Virgin Islands, and his first thought was: "The board was 5 feet, 10 inches by 21 or 22 inches wide, and I'm guessing about a foot thick? I'd never seen *any* board so thick, especially a Fish." David got to work on it, aided and abetted by his kids Luke and Luci (three and five years old) who helped with the color. Carson thought that might be cool, as he is a fan of kid art. Luke and Luci started with promising colors and shapes, but it turned to mud pretty quick. "It was a bit of a mess," he said, "so I stepped in later and added the white, to help give it more interest."

They did the top then the bottom. "He had done this kinda psychedelic sun, circle thing in greens and purples on the bottom and rails, and I thought the circle was just so cool. It was my inspiration. That and standing the board up before the paint had dried and enjoying seeing the too-thickly applied paint dribble down the board. I always loved the fact the top color design had nothing to do with the bottom, and vice versa. Two great, blank canvases to work with!"

Board courtesy David Carson and the Surfrider Foundation

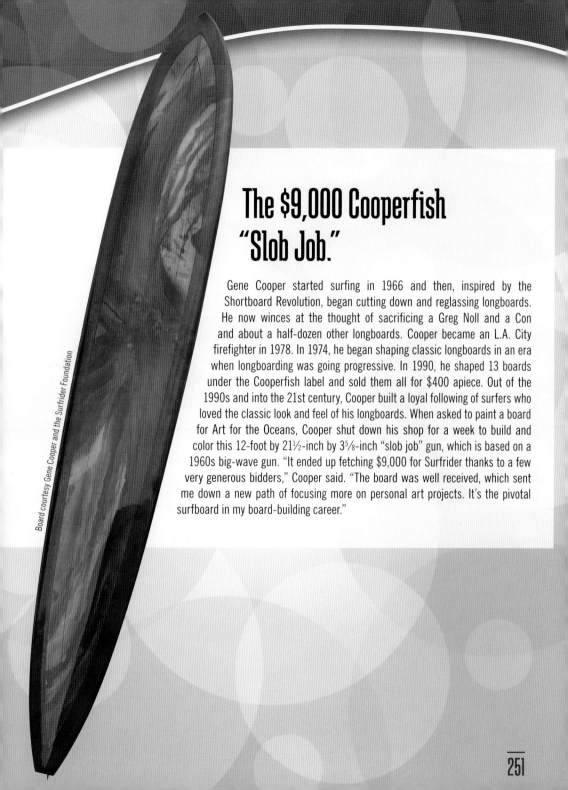

The $9,000 Cooperfish "Slob Job."

Gene Cooper started surfing in 1966 and then, inspired by the Shortboard Revolution, began cutting down and reglassing longboards. He now winces at the thought of sacrificing a Greg Noll and a Con and about a half-dozen other longboards. Cooper became an L.A. City firefighter in 1978. In 1974, he began shaping classic longboards in an era when longboarding was going progressive. In 1990, he shaped 13 boards under the Cooperfish label and sold them all for $400 apiece. Out of the 1990s and into the 21st century, Cooper built a loyal following of surfers who loved the classic look and feel of his longboards. When asked to paint a board for Art for the Oceans, Cooper shut down his shop for a week to build and color this 12-foot by 21½-inch by 3⅝-inch "slob job" gun, which is based on a 1960s big-wave gun. "It ended up fetching $9,000 for Surfrider thanks to a few very generous bidders," Cooper said. "The board was well received, which sent me down a new path of focusing more on personal art projects. It's the pivotal surfboard in my board-building career."

Board courtesy Gene Cooper and the Surfrider Foundation

Juanito Pelota's Gun Fish

Flip through gomezbueno.com, and you'll find all kinds of cool stuff from the mind to the hands of Gomez Bueno. For this Art for the Oceans board, Bueno painted one of his favorite characters, Juanito Pelotas, hugging a beautiful lady and holding a gun, in the style of a movie poster for a film entitled *Beaver Poison*. "For years I've been painting fictitious movie posters," he said. "This is one more piece of that collection only on a twin fin instead of a canvas."

Board courtesy Gomez Bueno and the Surfrider Foundation

Bethany Hamilton's One-Hand Board

Bethany Hamilton was 13 years old when she lost her arm to a tiger shark while surfing on the north shore of Kauai. That was more than a little inconvenient to a young girl who loved to surf and had the potential to join the Irons Brothers and Rochelle Ballard and many other great surfers from Kauai.

Bethany didn't give up, and Matt Biolos faced the challenge of making a special board. "I shaped this board like a year after she was attacked," Biolos said. The board is 5 feet, 10 inches long by 18¾ inches wide and 2¼ inches thick. Biolos said it was built in XTR construction, "a combination of extruded EPS 'XPS' foam and epoxy resin combined to make Bethany a very light board, in contrast to the extra foam volume she needed to catch waves while paddling with only one arm. The board features a special rope and rubber handle created and made by her brother and father. She uses these handles to 'duck dive' or push through waves."

On this board, just 18 months after losing her arm, Bethany won the Explorer Women's Division at the 2005 National Scholastic Surfing Association National Championships at Lower Trestles in San Clemente.

Courtesy Matt Biolos

Ned Evans's
Quasi-African Shield/Surfboard

Ned Evans is a Burbank-born, Venice and Malibu-based surfer/photographer/artist who received both his MFA and his BFA from UC Irvine in the 1970s. Evans describes himself as an abstract artist, and he has been involved in dozens of solo and group exhibitions over the past five decades.

Asked to paint a Fish for the Surfrider Foundation, Ned did this one. "I took the board as a shaped canvas, a totality," he said. "Rather than put a picture on the board I just approached the shape as a whole using a random grid similar to the abstract paintings I was doing at the time. In black and white—and due to the strength of the outline shape—I sort of ended up with a quasi-African shield /surfboard. Which was just fine with me." The board ended up perfectly complementing the lines and art of a home in Montauk, New York.

2005 Agave Ferrari

This beautiful replica of a 10-foot, 11-inch gun is a Ferrari made of agave. The board was originally glued up by Dr. Mark Bracker for Pat Curren to shape. But Curren wasn't available, so Gary Linden stepped in. Linden couldn't recall when he shaped the board, but he knew that the stringers were made of purple heart wood and the rest was made of agave. "Pat Curren is the big-wave shaper/surfer that I most admire," Linden said, "and it was a true honor to attempt a replica of his work."

Photo by Juliana Morais; Board courtesy Fernando Aguerre

Peace, Love, Life, Surf

Sometimes the cease and desist letters go the other way. Robb Havassy's board for Art for the Oceans combines themes that he has applied to other surfboards. The "peace, love, life, surf" and the kiss imagery were blended to create the aesthetic of this surfboard. According to Havassy, the "SURF Shield" came from a surfboard that was ripped off by Abercrombie & Fitch for their Hollister Co. brand. The faux surf-apparel company pirated Havassy's design by producing 365 replicas of his surfboard, including his signature, and making it the cornerstone for the look and vibe of their Hollister stores.

A two-year copyright infringement lawsuit ensued, which Robb opted to settle rather than waste precious time and money on appeals by the billion dollar corporation. "I got out at the perfect time," Havassy said. "I got 'em without losing my soul and a decade of my life in the process." Since settling the suit in 2007, Havassy has distributed more than 200 of those 365 surfboards to charities and collectors—making it one of the most collected surfboards ever.

Board courtesy Robb Havassy and the Surfrider Foundation

Garrett's Big Wave Quiver

Garrett McNamara, exuberant practitioner of big-wave surfing, makes do with either his bare hands or towing in behind an internal combustion machine. That's Garrett standing with the world famous Dick Brewer, who made the tow board McNamara rode to glory at Nazare, Portugal. According to Garrett's spokeswoman and comely companion Nicole, the board between McNamara and Brewer in the photo is the "Nazare Special," a 6-footer shaped by Brewer in 2007. The two boards on the right and left of them are 10-foot, 6-inch boards shaped by Brewer for McNamara to use in the Eddie Aikau Big Wave Invitational.

Nazare is a beach in Portugal that is to McNamara what the white whale was to Captain Ahab. He has been on the trail of the illusive 100-foot wave, and he has gotten close a couple of times at Nazare—with his feet strapped into that 6-foot Brewer and going like the devil as an ocean avalanche nips at his heels. Garrett just likes catching big waves.

Photos courtesy Garrett McNamara

The Obama Board

In 2008, Fernando Aguerre had the first of three "bro downs" with everyone's favorite styling bodysurfer: President Barrack Obama. Fernando has a photo of Obama signing his "Obama Surfs" T-shirt, and he also has this one-of-a-kind-board intended for the president's first election campaign. The board was shaped by Rusty Priesendorfer, whose big R logo also stood for Republican. In 2008, Rusty decided to support then-Senator Obama's presidential bid. The fundraising committee could not take in-kind donations, so Rusty was stuck with a very nice board, shaped by him and painted by a famous NASCAR race car painter from San Diego. "Incredible art," Fernando said, "with the flag stripes behind peeling waves and the same artwork on the other side of the board. The board sat at Rusty's for a few weeks, until I found out about it. I offered to buy it, we agreed on the price, Rusty got the money, and then he donated it to the Obama campaign. And I got one of the rarest and most unusual boards in history, the one and only 'Obama surfboard by Rusty.'"

Photo by Lucia Griggi

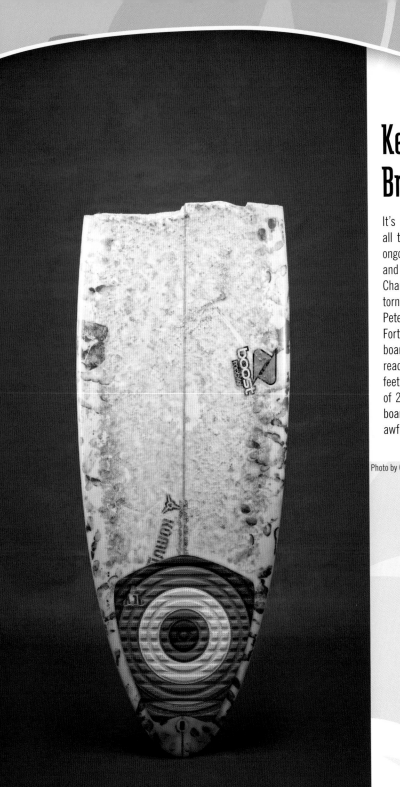

Kelly Slater's Broken Lance

It's a good thing Kelly Slater wins all those trophy boards and has an ongoing bro deal with Al Merrick and Channel Islands, because the Champ goes through surfboards like tornados go through trailer parks and Pete Townsend goes through guitars. Fortunately, the bottom half of this board remains, and it's possible to read the dimensions off the foam: 6 feet by 18⅜ inches with a thickness of 2⅝ inches. Slater was riding this board in 2008 at the age of 36; it's an awfully thin board for a grown man.

Photo by Chris Park; Board courtesy Bird's Surf Shed

Glass Slipper Bead Board

Creating and decorating surfboards can be a painstaking and fastidious process. Fernando Aguerre bought this board at Billabong's 2008 The Art of Shaping, Hawaii. This 7-foot Town and Country Glass Slipper mini-gun was shaped by Glenn Pang, who used tweezers to inlay—one by one—an estimated 35,000 to 40,000 ⅛-inch square glass beads into the deck of the board. The process took 100 hours over three weeks. The Art of Shaping was a fundraiser for the Liquid Nation Ball, chaired by Aguerre, to benefit 12 surf-based humanitarian organizations that have distributed $1.6 million dollars over eight years.

Photo by Lucia Griggi; Board courtesy Fernando Aguerre

Photo by Michael Williams; Board courtesy Gina Bradley and paddlediva.com

Gina Bradley's Paddle Diva SUP

Gina Bradley stands with the 2012 version of her Paddle Diva standup paddleboard. Bradley teaches standup paddling on Long Island when it's not iced over and flies south to Puerto Rico for the winter. In 2009 she designed the DIVA Stand Up Paddle Board for women, and this board is a 2012 modification on the design. Unlike many of the popouts from the east, this board is handcrafted by Mike Becker of Nature Shapes out of Sayville, Long Island. Dimensions are 10 feet by 29 inches by 3½ inches thick. "It's got a perfect design for riding a wave," Bradley said, "although we eliminated some of the traditional surfing features from it: chine edge, the bottom is flat with only a slight concave and we eliminated the nose rocker. It was built to be light and easy to manage so as to attract more women to the sport of SUP."

2009 Pipe Master Trophy Board

Phil Roberts's Pipe Masters trophy went around from his Newport Beach studio to Jeff Divine at *The Surfer's Journal* and finally into the hands of 2009 Pipe Masters champion Taj Burrow. The board is a 7-foot, 2-inch, rounded pintail single-fin Pipeliner Gun shaped by Gerry Lopez. "I used a Jeff Divine photo as a reference," Roberts said. "The art was under-painted with a freehand airbrush and then finished in acrylics on the sanded hotcoat deck. On the red-glassed bottom the Lightning Bolt is done in gold leaf, along with Gerry Lopez's signature."

Photo by Kirstin Scholtz/ASP via Getty Images

Photo by Melody Owens; Board courtesy Phil Roberts

261

Gally-Designed Santa Cruz Surfboards PT Stylemaster

Designed by Chris Gallagher with art by Lucas Musgrave and Peter "PT" Townend, this Santa Cruz Surfboards 6-foot, 2-inch by 19½-inch by 2.69-inch Stylemaster is the modern replica of a board used in the 1970s by Townend, the first professional surfing champion. The company's description of the board is enthusiastic: "Peter 'PT' Townend is a true stylemaster. A part of the original 'Bronzed Aussies' crew that lived on the North Shore of Oahu throughout the 70's. Known for wearing all pink, PT was surfing's first World Champion. This was during an era when shortboard surfing began to dominate the water as these pioneers experimented with new shapes that worked better in the powerful Hawaiian juice. Updated from his original templates and existing boards he shaped back in the day . . . the prototypes were tested in PT's original hometown of Coolangatta at the 'Superbank' and now come to you in the Powerlyte construction."

Courtesy Santa Cruz Surfboards

2012 Beer Can Surfboard

Yeah, the Beer Can Surfboard: a board using beer cans as a core and glassed and rideable. How cool is that? This board is on display at Bird's Surf Shed, but Rich Morrison sent proud, personal images of the board he created with help from Gary Seagraves. He also provided context for the 6-foot, 2-inch-long, 21-inch-wide Fish: "The born on date is 2011. . . . It's made of 72 recycled beer cans of six different brands: Bud, Modello, Rolling Rock, Boddingtons, Primo, and PBR." The board is 2¾-inch—the diameter of a beer can—and has two bamboo stringers, glassed-on twin fins, a beer-can channel bottom, and single beer-can wings. Some foam rounds out the shape. The board was surfed twice: once at Blacks Beach and once at Uppers, according to Morrison. "It's one of the most unique boards ever made and has huge appeal even to nonsurfers," he said. "It gets more photo love and attention at Bird's than all the boards in the Shed."

Photos courtesy Rich Morrison; Board courtesy Rich Morrison and Bird's Surf Shed

Tony Arruza Surfboard Project

Tony Arruza is a photographer and fine artist from West Palm Beach, Florida, who has been combining commercial photography with surf photography for more than 30 years. In 2010 he launched the Surfboard Art Project with the goal of bringing together traditional craftsmen who hand shape custom surfboards and the photographs from Arruza's archive. "Together we collaborate and combine our talents," he said. "The results are exquisitely crafted, aesthetically pleasing surfboards with a laminated pigment-ink print."

Arruza's goal is to produce 15 boards by 15 shapers. Here are three:

Pipeline is a McTavish-influenced 7-foot, 6-inch board shaped by Steve Firogenis of Firo Surfboards. The board has a photographic print of Pipeline on a polyester textile material glassed onto the foam and then is fiberglassed over.

Sunrise Lines features a photo from Durban, South Africa, on a 7-foot, 6-inch One World Surfboard shaped by Juan Rodriguez. The board is solid balsa with a redwood/birch wood nose and tail block. Fins are also made of redwood and birch wood laminates and are glassed on. The photographic print was inlaid with resin on top of the balsa before the board was glassed.

Legends in the Dark is an 8-foot, 6-inch board shaped by Jesse Fernandez for Wave Riding Vehicles Surfboards in 2012. The photo was taken on the North Shore in the 1980s, when most Hawaiian surfers were riding single fins. The traditional foam and resin board is a throwback to that era.

The Night Stalker

Humans are not apex predators at night, nor in the ocean, so night surfing combines chills with thrills, perils with pleasures. The Night Stalker is an S-wing shortboard with two adjustable 700-lumen headlamps mounted on a bar at the front—just behind a plexiglass viewing window so you can see what lies beneath, if you dare. The headlamps are powered by rechargeable batteries waterproofed within the board. The side fins also have LED lights, that must look cool or spooky from under water and will either attract big fish or scare them off. What lies beneath the board is an arty tribute to Thomas Edison and also the team of seven who made the board. The board was auctioned at Billabong's Art of Shaping charity event, with the proceeds sent off to the 2010 SIMA Humanitarian Fund.

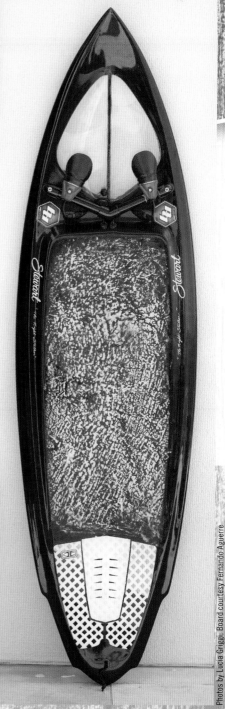

Photos by Lucia Griggi. Board courtesy Fernando Aguerre

2010 Pipe Masters Trophy Board

These trophy boards are pretty sweet, no? The 7-foot, 2-inch rounded pintail single fin is the kind of board Gerry Lopez rode to glory during his Glory Days in the 1970s—a simple, clean design refined by many, many days at the Pipeline. Phil Roberts used a Jeff Divine photo of Lopez riding a 7-foot, 2-inch rounded pintail single fin. He freehanded the airbrush, underpainting on the raw foam, and then painted details in oils on the sanded hotcoat deck. "The bottom of the board was first glassed red for a base then gold leafed over the whole thing," Roberts said. "Any natural cracks or artist flaws in the gold leaf panels and the red would show through—giving it a vintage, handcrafted, Italian frieze kind of look. Wrapping that gold leaf cleanly around the rails is a trick to do." Well, surfing Pipeline and Backdoor is a tricky thing, too, and 22- year-old Jeremy Flores did both well to defeat Kieren Perrow to win the 40th Billabong Pipe Masters in Honor of Andy Irons to take this trophy board back to France.

2011 Pipe Masters Trophy Board

Kieren Perrow must have taken it personally when he finished runner up to Jeremy Flores at the 2010 Pipeline Masters in Memory of Andy Irons. So he came back the next year and won the whole deal. For his skill and daring, Perrow took home $75,000 and this trophy board, shaped by Gerry Lopez and painted by Phil Roberts. Roberts took a raw 7-foot, 2-inch rounded pintail single fin and airbrushed a Brian Bielmann image of Andy Irons doing a grab-rail bottom turn at Pipeline. So an image of someone other than Gerry Lopez was a departure from the previous boards, and this 2011 version is also different because Roberts used silver leaf on the bottom and the rail rap.

Walden's 1975 Pre-Magic Longboard

Steve Walden began production shaping in 1968, at 20 years old, for Greek Surfboards in Huntington Beach, California. He went into business himself the following year, and within four years he was one of the largest surfboard producers in the United States. After moving to Hawaii in 1972, he produced boards for Lightning Bolt, Surfline Hawaii, and Hawaiian Island Creations. As the Shortboard Revolution was raging in 1973, Walden integrated the speed and maneuverability of a shortboard into a weight-reduced longboard. Walden breathed life back into the longboard and supercharged it.

In 1981, Walden returned to California, where he created the Magic Model and now operates out of Ventura. He shaped this board, which he is holding in front of his shop, in 1975 for himself. The 9-foot by 22½-inch by 3-inch board was carved from a regular polyurethane blank. "This board is very special to me," Walden said. "Back at Rocky Point, when I was developing the modern longboard—which eventually became the Original Magic Model—I was experimenting with the design, and this board was one of the first boards that, when I was done, I knew I was on to something magical. Thus the name. I surfed Rocky Point at least twice a day and this was my go-to board. Every Magic Model that has been built since can trace its roots back to this board."

Photos by Elizabeth Pepin

Nobby's Hobby

Nobuhito "Nobby" Ohkawa is a resident of Chiba, Japan, who has been crafting beautiful wooden surfboards going back to 2007. A trip to Infinity Surfboards in California inspired Nobby to start shaping and glassing, and then he turned to wood. He makes boards from Paulownia, the same wood Tom Wegener uses in Australia. "My philosophy is preserve nature in the surfboards, and I think it's the significance to wooden surfboards," Nobby said. "That's why I have been making surfboards with wood, so natural touch and very smooth ride." That's Nobby's 9-foot, 8-inch by 23-inch by 3¼-inch Woodslider standing in a stand of trees and a 6-foot by 21-inch by 3-inch single fin he shaped in 2010.

Cornwall Grains

Six thousand miles away from Chiba, Japan, Mark Roberts at Glass Tiger Surfboards has been handcrafting beautiful surfboards out of wood for about as long as Nobby. Roberts's boards have cores made from EPS (expanded polystyrene) foam, but the boards are wrapped in a variety of veneers and hardwoods. The deck and bottom are skinned in 1.5 mm structural veneers bonded to the foam core with glass cloth and epoxy. Roberts generally uses Cornish ash and chestnut for the rails. The nose and tail blocks are reinforced with Iroko wood to resist dings. Each board has a vent,

like the Tom Blake paddleboards of old. And like the days of old, Roberts feels his boards are tough enough that they need no lamination—no resin and fiberglass to protect the wood. He coats them with multiple layers of varnish, and that's that.

Huck's *Shoji* Board

In 2011, Neal "Huck" Bahrman spent six months handcrafting this 7-foot, 4-inch by 21-inch by 2½-inch Egg. "Craftsmen once made functional objects of great beauty, treasured for generations," Huck said, "and it seemed to me that in our mass-production world of disposable objects, such craftsmen are becoming an endangered species. I wanted to make an artistic statement that honored that handcrafted tradition."

Huck was inspired by the Japanese *shoji*, which are windows, doors, or room dividers made of translucent paper held together by a lattice of wood or bamboo. "I created a structural geometric framework, over which I applied a skin of polyester fabric," Huck said. "Using artist's tissue, the board was embellished with a koi fish, a motif popular on Japanese kites, and the Japanese Kanji symbol for *shoji*. On the deck are the symbols for 'respect' and 'craftsman.'"

Of course, paper isn't going to hold up in the sun and the surf, so Huck turned to plastics. "I finished up with two layers of fiberglass and epoxy resin, and a leash anchor and vent (to be closed when the board is in the water, and opened when on dry land, due to the contraction and expansion of the air inside). Set up as a quad, the board has interior support for a single-fin box if desired."

While being used as a not-for-sale display in a retail environment, the board was sold to a patron of the arts.

Photos by Neal "Huck" Bahrman

Photo by Kevin Roche

Heather's Feathers

She's a lovely girl who likes to paint lovely girls and mermaids and dreamy, ocean-inspired art on surfboards. Heather Ritts started painting surfboards in high school through the tiny Lost shop on the Pacific Coast Highway in San Clemente. Airbrusher Tom "Suds" Sutherland took her under his wing as an associate artist, and she met a lot of the surfboard makers in the San Clemente "surf ghetto." "I paint boards, fins, and everything in between," Ritts said. "I paint on wood and board in oil when not painting boards. I am lucky to have been included in several surf art shows and other events. Recently I was included in the Board Art Benefit with some really incredible artists and continue to paint on a daily basis."

Boards courtesy Heather Ritts

Sage's Surfboard Art

Brian Sage grew up in a small New England town in Connecticut and showed an early affinity for art, which was encouraged by his mother and grandfather, both accomplished artists. Sage earned a degree in fine arts at Rollins College and then wandered a bit before settling down and taking his art seriously as a career. Sage describes himself as an American Impressionist whose focus is on people and their relationship to one another and their surroundings.

Sage likes to surround himself in the ocean and waves and one sideline to his art involves turning surfboards into works of art. Sage takes quality surfboards and then applies Modern Impressionist scenes from the surfing world and even as far inland as Las Vegas.

Photos by Mat Arney; Boards courtesy James Otter

James Otter's Cornish "Jetty"

Remember, it was British craftsmanship that made the sailing vessels that transported Captain Cook all the way from England and halfway around the world to the South Pacific, where he and his crew saw the first wave riders and commented on "the most supreme pleasure." James Otter finds that making modern surfboards from wood is supremely pleasurable as well. In the summer of 2011, Otter worked with photographer Mat Arney to take a series of photographs on the "Storyboard," which followed the process of making a wooden board from felling the trees to finished product. The board they made they called "the Jetty," which is their version of the classic Egg shape. The board is 6 feet, 10 inches by $2\frac{5}{8}$ inches, all built from Cornish western red cedar in a skin-and-frame construction method. "The significance of the board is that it shows how we can use modern processes coupled with sustainable materials," Otter said, "or about as sustainable as materials can get—gotta love wood—to create highly functional surfboards that will last a lifetime."

The three boards against the barn include Big Blue, a finished version of the Jetty model, and Otter's take on the Lis Fish.

Spacek's Blue Fish Board

Artist Peter Spacek is a resident of Montauk, Long Island, at the end of a peninsula that pokes way out into the Atlantic and is visited by a wide variety of ocean species, from white sharks to blue fish. The blue fish is a popular fish for ocean sport-fishing, but they can be a little hazardous when they are in the middle of a blitz (feeding frenzy) and swimmers or surfers are in the middle of that blitz. Spacek was once fishing in the middle of a blue fish blitz, and a fish he caught got payback by biting his thumb.

So, Peter and blue fish have a history, and Spacek laid down this tribute to the toothy blitzer on a 6-foot, 10-inch Bulkley that Spacek had taken around the world in 1992. Spacek had been experimenting with scrimshawing images into surfboard fiberglass then rubbing ink into the fine lines. "The technique was well suited to detailed rendering of fins and scales, so I pulled the nicely patinaed Bulkley off the wall and imagined a slightly distorted bluefish, the length of the board, about to bite down on the Bulkley decal on the nose. The technique is fairly physical and slow, so it took about a month to do, and I really don't think it's done yet, but this is it for now. It's all about the eye with the bluefish, it looks fierce and smart. Striped bass eyes don't look like that—they're called cows. I'll take a bluefish over a bass any day."

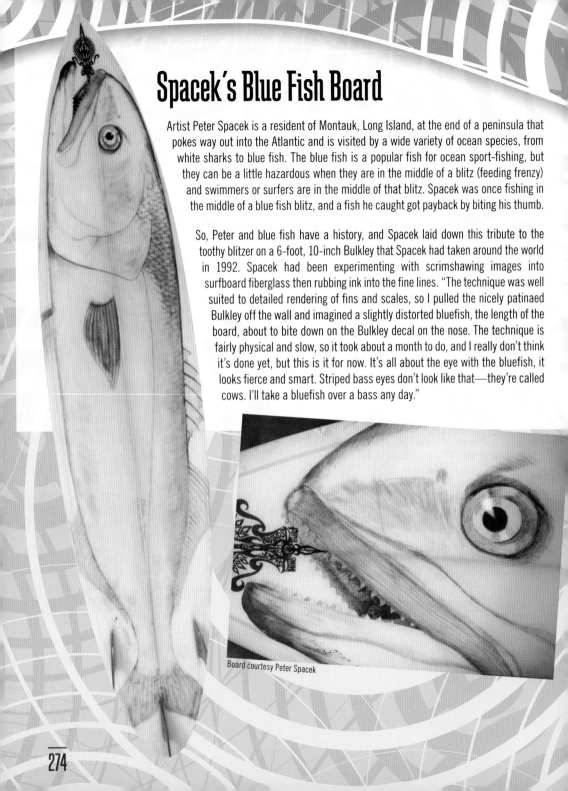

Board courtesy Peter Spacek

John Whitmer's Compsand Balsa Boards

Originally from the east coast of Florida, John Whitmer wanted something completely different. He couldn't move to New Zealand, but he looked at the climate, surf, topography, and rural outlook of Oregon and gave it a try. He ended up in the booming metropolis of Beaver, Oregon (population 125). A boat builder by trade, Whitmer figured if he could build a $13 million, 65-foot wood sport fishing yacht, he could build boards. He started with two traditional chambered balsa guns and now 25 years and almost 400 boards later, he is working at the cutting edge of the industry's underground design/construction fringe.

Whitmer specializes in what he calls compsand boards, which means "composite sandwich." The three boards in the photo are, from left: a 9-foot by 20-inch by 21-pound balsa gun shaped in 1998 from imported Ecuadorian balsa and local Pacific Northwest redwood; a 7-foot, 6-inch by 9.1 pound compsand with balsa bottom, balsa and D'cell rails, and caramel bamboo deck; and a 6-foot by 21-inch by 7.2-pound balsa composite sandwich Quad Fish shaped in 2013.

Boards courtesy John Whitmer

The Leenough

Marc Andreini's 5-foot, 5-inch Leenough Quad is a standup version of Greenough's Velo kneeboard made for Bob Leonelli, an Andreini team rider since 1972. "Leo rides this board everywhere between Santa Cruz and San Diego. The best it ever worked was at a perfect 6-foot day at Rincon where he made two waves from the top of the point to the freeway," Andreini said. "Making a standup version of Velo is what fueled 100 percent of the performance shortboard revolution. I am just one of many who surfed with George and wanted to adopt his approach. In reality George has stated that he can only give suggestions and that the rider must adjust and fine-tune his own board because standing has an entirely different effect than kneeling on the board's performance. This version is the best working one I ever came up with thanks to the quad-fin setup, which solves the wide tail block side slip problem of early single fin attempts."

Nova Scocean

Nova Scotia artist Daina Scarola likes to oil paint surf art, and during the summer of 2012, she had the opportunity to paint a beautiful handcrafted cedar strip 6-foot swallowtail shaped by Alex Hanssen of Henning Shapes. "I painted the board last summer," Scarola said. "But I think Alex made it a couple years before that. He built it to ride it, but it was so heavy in the end. He was still determined to take it out, and if I remember correctly, he surfed it three times. The last time he realized it was either going on the wall or he had a death wish. But then, Alex trains for Skeleton, a winter Olympic sport similar to luge, but instead of a team of sledders, you're solo going down head first on a superfast curvy ice track. Kinda crazy!"

Courtesy Daina Scarola, www.oceanartstudio.ca

Honest Abe Board

Orange County to Los Angeles artist Damian Fulton showed up to the 2011 Sacred Craft Art Show at Del Mar, California, with this 8-foot, 4-inch single-fin gun shaped by Tyler Hatzikian and got to work. Over two days, Fulton systematically applied metallic enamel spray and India ink to the deck, painting the board in such a way that no one could really tell what he was imagining. After two days of hard work and gawkers, Fulton finally connected the dots and revealed a beautiful portrait of the 16th U.S. president. From far away, it's cool. From close, it's cooler: Lincoln's right eye is made up of sea creatures, women's footwear, and other fine details. The board sold for $3,495.

Board and photos courtesy Damian Fulton

Allen Lassiter's Balsa Board

Balsa is light because most of the cells are full of air—but is balsa lighter than air? Allen Lassiter engaged in some photographic hijinks to show off this 6-foot, 4-inch (on the long rail) asymmetrical balsa board he displayed in Cowboy Bob's booth at The Boardroom show in Del Mar, California, in October 2012. "I had the balsa for the better part of 15 years," Lassiter said, "just collecting dust and getting a few worm holes when I finally got shamed into making a board out of it. Robert 'Cowboy Bob' Rudine gave me some redwood for stringers (I sent him a case of Tiger Beer in return). I offset the center redwood stringer with some Paulownia. A true multicultural board: it's got koa for a tailblock, balsa from Ecuador, redwood stringers from Norcal, and Paulownia from North Carolina." The finished product came in at around 10 pounds. But is that lighter than air? The photo was taken by David Bright using a bit of fishing line for levitation.

Photo by David Bright; board courtesy Allen Lassiter

Zatarra's Chocolaty Goodness

This surfboard that looks like an exotic chocolate confection is actually a handmade hollow wooden board that Neal "Huck" Bahrman calls Zatarra, from a line in the movie *Count of Monte Cristo*. According to Huck, the visual inspiration was a large piece of driftwood at Malibu Beach by the First Point lifeguard tower, and shaping the board was a time-consuming project that took nine months to complete. It is a 7-foot by 22-inch by 2¾-inch rebuild of a single fin Egg made with wood rails and a foam middle. "I removed the foam middle, kept the rails, hollowed them out, and started over," Huck explained. "Second in a series of boards designed to be handcrafted in a way that no machine could ever duplicate! In addition to the driftwood-inspired swirls, I also let the stringer show—for no good reason other than I hadn't seen it done on a hollow wood surfboard before."

Photos by Neal "Huck" Bahrman

The Huichol Bead Board

The millenary Huichol Indians live in the Sierra Madre Occidental Mountains of Central Mexico. They have been doing art with beads for centuries. This particular board was especially commissioned by a Mexican friend of Fernando Aguerre and presented as a gift. The board uses 170,000 beads glued to beeswax to depict traditional Huichol art along with surfing scenes. The board took over a month of nonstop beading and is very beautiful when viewed close up. This is one of only two in the world.

Photo by Lucia Griggi; Board courtesy Fernando Aguerre

CEO Surfboard

Paul Naude is a South African pro surfer who has been an executive for Billabong since 1998. Running a billion-dollar business is relentless work, but Naude had the time to recycle a longboard from Joel Tudor and reshape it into this modern hull, with art applied by Andy Davis. The current owner Fernando Aguerre said that, in addition to shaping the board, Naude glassed it as well—"an art most probably lost by most surf industry CEOs," Aguerre added.

Photo by Lucia Griggi; Board courtesy Fernando Aguerre

2012 Pipe Trophy Board

Getting tired of looking at these Pipe Masters trophy boards yet? Nope. They're beautiful. The painting of a guy paddling out at Pipe comes from a Brian Bielmann photo. Roberts freehand airbrushed the painting on the foam deck then used oils to paint details on the sanded hotcoat deck. The bottom is a candy cobalt blue tint finish with a clear gloss coat with silver leaf rail rap, and the Lightning Bolt glistens with gold leaf. Joel Parkinson took this home, along with the 2012 World Title.

Board courtesy Phil Roberts

Roseman's Quiver

Jon Roseman divides his time between the reefs of La Jolla and the reefs of Tavarua Island in Fiji. And he has a different quiver of boards for each. The four red Bessell boards below make up Roseman's selection for surfing around La Jolla. And that's him stripped down and battle ready with a Fish and five boards for surfing Tavarua from 2 feet to 20.

Photo courtesy Jon Roseman

Pleydell-Pearce's Painted *Paipos*

Remember back in the 1930s when Bert Yeo was the bellyboard king of Woolacombe, England? That mantle seems to have passed to Steve Pleydell-Pearce, a 21st century resident of Woolacombe who makes and paints very cool bellyboards for friends and family. About these boards, Pleydell-Pearce explained: "In the spring of 2012, I made the two big boards, which are 48 inches by 24 inches by ¼ inch, from marine plywood, varnish, and embellished with acrylic paint. The PP Lobster is a crossover between a traditional English bellyboard, a Hawaiian *paipo*, and a fishtail surfboard. The boards are flat for speed and have a big fish tail for hanging in steep low-tide drops and speedy walls: no tailspins on cranking bottom turns."

Athena's Mean Green

Athena Shlien is Queen of the Rock, but that's all we're gonna say about the semisecret spot she surfs somewhere in Malibu. She loves cats and playing drums and hiking in the Santa Monica Mountains and taking sexual photos of flowers. And she also loves this 5-foot, 8-inch surfboard, which she got in 2013. "There is some history to this board," Athena said. "But I don't know if I can tell it. I used to ride a Rusty Piranha—that's a board made by Rusty called a Piranha. So I took that to Glenn Kennedy who shapes boards over in the Valley, on Ventura Boulevard. I said, 'I love this board. It's my favorite board, but I want one that's a little more hydrodynamic. A little faster.' Glenn said the Piranha was originally his design, and I hope that doesn't cause any trouble with Rusty. So he made me a board, and I like it better than my Rusty Piranha. I love it because it paddles fast and it rides super superfast. It gets me around sections, and it's pretty maneuverable."

Photo by Lucia Griggi

Bending Balsa in Bend

Dave Town is a balsa bender who lives in Bend, Oregon. Like a lot of surfboard shapers going back to the 1930s, Town loves the look and feel of balsa and the satisfaction of carving perfection from those buttery planks. He shaped a 12-foot by 23-inch by 3-inch board based on a Skip Frye Glider, and it weighed in at 32 pounds. "I made the blank from 12-foot solid balsa lumber," Town said. "Scarfed the boards to achieve the correct rocker. I used spot glue and all-thread to hold the board together during the initial rough shaping. Prior to final sanding, I broke the board down into individual pieces to be chambered. After chambering the board was glued up and glassed. Redwood stringer glassed with 6 ounce top and bottom. The board was designed to be surfed with my kids on small summertime waves."

The shorter board—9 feet by 22¼ inches by 3 inches—is also very heavy and is based on a 1958 balsa Velzy Pig. "I made that board in 2011 for myself, friends, and anyone who wants to surf it," Town said. "It's solid balsa with a koa wood fin. Glassed with 4 ounce, top and bottom. This was my first balsa-constructed board."

Boards courtesy Dave Town

English Geometry

The English didn't stop making cool surfboards in the 1980s. These boards are from Circle One, but they have more than one circle and other geometric shapes. Shaped in 2013 the boards are all 7-foot, 6-inch by 21¾-inch by 2½-inch round pintails. The art was laid down by Luke Finch, aka WeLoveNoise. "I designed the board's artwork to act more as a piece of art with meaning and connection to the surf culture," he explained. "On a more sentimental level, these were also the first boards I designed for the surf industry, so they obviously hold a special place in my heart."

The *Contour* is a geometrical impression of a wave base. It is the maximum depth at which a water wave's passage causes significant water motion. *Stark* reflects the rigorous motion of a wave. Sharply clear; impossible to avoid. As for the circles in *Orbital*, when a wave passes, water particles are moved in a circular orbital motion. The radius of the circle of motion for any given water molecule decreases exponentially with increasing depth.

Forever Stoked's 21-Board Salute

That's Chris Pedersen getting all Busby Berkeley, surrounded by a 21-board salute to the LA Lakers, Rick Griffin, Dr. Seuss, Salvador Dali, and God knows what else. The boards were shaped by Shane Stoneman, Jerry Grantham, PJ Wahl, and Dev and Chris Borst in lengths from 5 feet, 10 inches to 7 feet, 10 inches and all were painted by Pedersen before being ridden. "Hopefully people enjoy seeing the paint jobs in the water," Pedersen said. "Often people think they are just for display. But all are painted as a tribute to Mother Nature, and they have all been in the barrel!"

The *Angler Fish* was shaped in 2011 by Peter Pierce for himself at 5 feet, 4 inches by 18¾ inches by 2¼ inches. Pierce also did the artwork. "The 'pod/wizard sleeve' style boards were trendy at the time, so I wanted to try something similar but different. I had also wanted to build a unique Bonzer. So, I merged the ideas and came up with this board. . . . It can also maneuver really well in a tight pocket. I've had some incredible sessions on it. I've also had some horrible sessions as well. It doesn't have hardly any volume, so it paddles slow, and bigger days meant lots of missed waves."

Grommet Comet

The Australian word *grom* is short for "grommet" and is what Aussies call a young surfer. It's a derivation of the American word for a young surfer: "gremlin/gremmie." Or maybe it's vice versa. Anyway, Harry Bryant is a 5-foot, 10-inch by 16 years old by 64 kilogram (142 pound) grom from Noosa Heads who is a high-placing contender in the highly competitive Pro Junior series. Bryant is proud owner of a nine-board quiver, but the one in his hand is a 5-foot, 9-inch by 18¼-inch by 2¹/₁₆-inch board shaped by Al Emery of Emery Surfboards in Byron Bay. "I've been working with Al for about five years and he is really in-tune with what I'm looking for with my boards," Bryant said. "Having a good relationship with your shaper would have to be the key element in your surfing, so you can fine-tune every little detail in your boards and he can tell you what every little shape and curve can do to benefit your surfing."

The artwork is by Jake Donlen from Runamuk Visuals. "I always saw his designs on surfboards all over Noosa, and I always loved his artwork," Bryant said, "so I let him go mad on this latest batch of boards and they all turned up mental. This board has Set-Fins and a lighter glass job. It's so light and it's great in the small, fast waves around Noosa."

LSD Twinzer

David Levy shapes surfboards in Rhode Island under the LSD label, which translates to Levy Surf Designs. This is Levy's Twinzer, a 5-foot, 8-inch by 23-inch by 3-inch board that he made for himself. "It's made of 2-pound Styrofoam, Resin Research Kwick Kick Epoxy, and equipped with FCS Fusion plugs," Levy explained. "It was supposed to be a squash tail, but I decided to do a swallow tail to cut down on the sliding and give it more range. It's a good design if you don't want to ride a long board. Works great thru flat spots and is very fat and still pumps down the line. Floats a lot, so you can ride the board smaller. A lot of fun for the average waves we have in Rhode Island."

Vincenzo's Reincarnated Surfboard

The Italian Mediterranean can have surprisingly good surf, and some locations are spectacularly beautiful. Vincenzo Ganadu is an Italian surfer who likes to contribute to the beauty by painting his surfboards, and he is a big believer in recycling. This 6-foot by 19-inch by 2¼-inch shortboard was cut down from a 9-foot longboard shaped by Maurizio Rossi of WWB Surfboards. Ganadu got the longboard in 2002 and rode it in the points around northwest Sardinia at waves like Porto Ferro, Marritza, and also Argentiera. But the board was retired to the backyard where it got a nice suntan in the summer.

In 2012 and 2013, Priamo Frau of FX Surfboards shaped that longboard down and gave it new life. "The idea of recovering an old longboard that gave me so many emotions and make it living again in new shape and colors is a process of absolute respect and useful for us," said Ganadu. "I think many shapers should practice this form of reinventing their surfboards and recycling materials. It's also a good training for our minds and souls: we all heard the story that every board is already inside the materials (wood, foam, etc.). Now we are in the next level, that I call the reincarnation of surfboard. Who really knows what could be inside the boards you have in the garage?"

Allan Weisbecker's Mainland Mexico Special

Photo by Keith Novosel

Keith Novosel escaped the Portland winter and took a trip down to tropical climes, where he found author and adventurer Allan Weisbecker styling in his winter/spring getaway, a little bungalow he rents in Mexico. The 9-foot, 4-inch longboard was shaped by Jim Goldberg of Hook Surfboards. "It has a lot of rocker, a little concave in the nose, and a template loosely based on the old 50-50," Weisbecker said. When asked if there was anything special about materials or construction, he said: "I was there the whole time, annoying Jim with comments and suggestions. Is that special? I brought the board to Mexico, left it here, and only have ridden it here."

Photo by Elizabeth Pepin

Moses's Big Rig

Moses Paskowitz stands tall in front of a Big Rig Mickey Munoz 12-footer at the House of Flys Surf Shop in Waikiki. Moses is a Paskowitz, a family that is to surfing what the Jackson family is to music. There's a whole lotta Paskowitzes, and Moses is a big one, in heart and otherwise. For many years the Paskowitz *ohana* ran a surf school at San Onofre in California. Moses was born in Makaha, and like a salmon finding its way upriver, Moses moved back to Hawaii where he teaches surfing on the beach at Waikiki. Moses uses the Big Rig for training and for paddling bigger students.

Photo by Roberto Tolin

Tubercled Hydrofoils

Pablo Diaz is a hydrofoiler from Asturias in northern Spain. Hydrofoiling is a new kind of surfing in which the rider stands on a board attached to a small plane with two wings that ride under the surface of the water. Towed into a wave behind a PWC, the hydrofoiler lets go of the rope and lets the wings underwater tap into all that raw swell energy. The board Diaz rides is made of samba wood—4 feet, 10 inches by 16 inches by $1\frac{5}{8}$ inches—laminated with epoxy and two layers of 6 ounce fiberglass top and bottom with an additional two layers on the bottom tail area where the stress plate of the strut is attached. "It's pretty much built like a tank because the stresses on its tail are considerable," Diaz said. "And they take quite a beating on the ski in the long run.

"The board is connected to the wings through a 46-inch aluminum strut and a 36-inch aluminum fuselage, where they are fixed. All my wings are made of G-10 [a glass-reinforced epoxy laminate] and the main ones have had spans ranging from 24 inches to $29\frac{1}{2}$ inches, with chords from $4\frac{3}{4}$ inches to $6\frac{1}{2}$ inches and maximum thicknesses from 0.3937 inch to 0.59 inch. The latest one has a $25\frac{1}{2}$-inch span with a $6\frac{1}{2}$-inch chord and a 0.3937-inch maximum thickness."

The biggest innovation in Diaz's rig are the experimental "tubercled" wings. "Since 2010, I have been designing and building tubercled wings, based on recent research on the performance of humpback whales' pectoral fins. Studies have shown that this configuration orders flow, increasing angle of attack up to 40 percent and delaying stall, as well as reducing wing tip vortices and induced drag. Tubercled wings feel all around smoother and more forgiving than conventional ones, and their stall is more gradual and predictable."

Barry Snyder's Famous Faces

How good are you at attaching names to famous faces? Barry Snyder is a shaper/designer for Windigo Surfboards in Oceanside who thought it would be cool to paint a series of historic figures onto a line of surfboards. He was right. This is cool. Snyder worked for both Dick Brewer and Gary Linden for 16-plus years. And he's been an airbrush artist since he was a teen. He glues his own blanks and shapes them by hand—no computer shaping machines—and does all the artwork and glasses and sands most of them. The boards are all 5-foot, 8-inch to 6-foot, 2-inch with a couple of asymmetricals. Snyder painted them for the Boardroom Surfboard Show in Del Mar, California, in October 2012. "These portraits are the model names for the Windigo Surfboards line 2012," Snyder said. "All iconic figures from history. Mostly a rebel theme." Shown here are Franklin Roosevelt, Winston Churchill, Johnny Cash, General Douglas McArthur, Geronimo, General George Patton, John Wayne, Bronco Nagurski, and Pancho Villa.

Courtesy Barry Snyder

293

Firefighter Rink's Speed Machine

Gene Rink is an engineer for Los Angeles County Fire Station 88, located just behind the Malibu Colony and about half a mile from First Point Malibu. "Engineer" means Rink gets to drive the big red machine, a 28-foot, 7-inch by 100-inch wide (with mirrors) by 410 HP by 40,000 pound KME engine. Weaving that beast through traffic going Code Three on Pacific Coast Highway is excellent practice for surfing through the beastly crowds at First Point Malibu—one of the most crowded, chaotic surf spots in the world. For the surfing, Gene rides a replica of a 1980 Mark Richards Fish. "This was a board that MR used to win a championship," Rink said. "It's 5-foot, 10-inch by 20-inch board shaped by Scott Anderson at AquaTech. I have the Quad setup, and it's a super-fast speed machine."

Photo by Athena Shlien

Keith's Portland Plastic Posse

Keith Novosel lives in Portland, where he works for Lensbaby, maker of creative effects SLR lenses. The closest ocean is about an hour and a half drive away, but the Oregon Coast is active and has a variety of moods that require a variegated collection of boards. Novosel's collection includes (from left to right) a yellow and light blue-gray, 9-foot, 10-inch longboard shaped in 2009 by Griffin Neumann-Kyle of Almond Surfboards and Designs; a heart-red 8-foot, 9-inch board that Novosel shaped in 2011; a small red handplane made by Parrish Watts in 2010; a 6-foot, 9-inch gray Hull shaped in 2009 by Ryan Lovelace; a 5-foot, 5-inch pink Mini Simmons Quad Fish made in 2012 by Trey Edwards III of the Peninsula Holding Company; and two bellyboards by Parrish Watts of Vintage Pacific Surfcraft. And that is what the properly equipped, city-dwelling, surf-fiending gentlemen has on hand these days.

Photo by Keith Novosel

Boards courtesy Shawn Griggs

Shawn Griggs Art Boards

Shawn Griggs comes from way up in the Arctic latitudes of northern California, in a lovely little town called Ferndale. He's been making art since childhood, and in college, he focused on illustration and design, inspired by Arthur Rackham and Alphonse Mucha. "It wasn't until 1999 that I finally embraced the paintbrush," Griggs said, "and found that I enjoyed how forgiving painting was compared to the tight rigidness of drawing with pen and ink."

Here are some samples of Grigg's art: *Skeleton Puking Octopi and Flowers* was shaped by Tim Stamps in 2012 and painted by Griggs late that year; the board for *Flying Goat vs. Robo Jellies* was bought at a garage sale and painted in 2012; *The Robot with a Heart* was shaped in 2009 by Tim Gras and painted early in 2012; *The Red Devil Squid* board was shaped by local shaper Jesse Kinsella and painted 2013.

Shane McIntyre's One Possible Future Protest Board

This board was made in the late 1990s, but it's a glimpse of the future. Shane McIntyre is a traveling surfer/shaper who made this board somewhere between 1997 and 1999. He had made about 500 boards under the label Mac Surfboards but was feeling creatively restrained. "It wasn't a great time to be shaping in my opinion," McIntyre said. "Creativity was largely rejected—straight up laughed at, and it was rare to even shape/sell a Fish during this time. I started shaping because of the art of the craft, and in my mind, there were no parameters to board design. The more I felt this way the more confined my shaping became—fueled by orders of endless squash-tail-tri-con-potato-chip-Thrusters. I felt like a machine and thought KKL should be doing this not me."

McIntyre bailed out on shaping and the Mac label, but this was his goodbye. The board is safety orange as a warning sign that surfboard design should never be limited.

I.S.A. *Alaia*

This 6-foot balsa *alaia* was shaped by Rasty. No not Rusty, or Rasta; Rasty is a famous shaper and hotel owner in Montanita, Ecuador. Look closely, and you'll see the signatures of Layne Beachley, Allen Sarlo, Jim Hogan, and all the masters competing in the 2013 International Surfing Association Masters World Champs. "Glassed over signatures," owner Fernando Aguerre said. "Ready to be ridden."

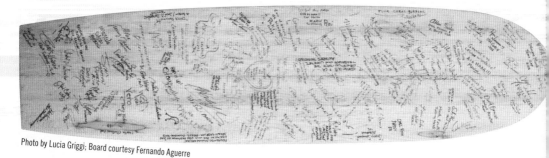

Photo by Lucia Griggi; Board courtesy Fernando Aguerre

Photo by Nelson Veiga; Boards courtesy Rosaldo Cavalcanti

Carioca Quiver

The RVCA on this man's chest stands for Rosaldo Very CariocA. Rosaldo Cavalcanti is a proud resident of Rio de Janeiro—journalist, surfer, promoter, and man about town. Rio is one of the most beautiful cities on the planet, between the jungle and the deep blue sea, and it's a city where everyone gets in the water. A true Carioca is ready for anything, and Rosaldo is equipped with two boards for when the surf is pumping or flat. The stand-up paddleboard is only 8 feet by 27½ inches and was shaped by Rosaldo's friend Kaneca. "Kaneca's a legend in Brazilian surfing," Rosaldo said. "He was not only the number-one shaper during the early '70s, but he also had the best chicks that used to hang out on Ipanema's Pier." Rosaldo's SUP is stringerless with carbon rails. "Everything is special about this board. It just makes me think that surfing is about having fun and I have a lot of fun riding it."

The shortboard is a 6-foot, 3-inch board shaped for Mark Occhiluppo, who gave it to Rosaldo as thanks for all the good times they had together in Rio. "All I know is that it works unreal! I trust this board in any kind of wave up to 6 feet."

Shawn Dollar's Cortes Killer

Photo by Nikki Brooks

In December of 2012, Shawn Dollar took a boat a hundred miles out to sea to a place called Cortes Bank. He paddled way up to the top of the reef and paddled into a moose of a wave on this board. It was shaped by Jason Stevens in 2012 based off of Dollar's 9-foot, 6-inch Mavericks boards. This one is 10 feet, 6 inches long and $3^{11}/_{16}$ inches thick, a Quad that was glassed twice and weighs about 25 pounds. "I surfed the biggest wave of my life on it during that paddle session at Cortes Bank on December 21, 2012," Dollar recalled. "It's up for the XXL biggest paddle. Many are calling it a new world record, but I'm waiting to find out."

As it turned out, on May 3, 2013, the judges for the Billabong XXL Big Wave awards took a close look at a lot of contenders and decided Shawn Dollar paddled into a wave at Cortes Bank that measured 61 feet—earning it both the Pacifico Paddle Champion and the 2013 XXL Biggest Wave Champion—and earning the surfer a tidy $35,000. It was that thick 10-foot, 6-inch board that got him there. "The board was shaped for paddling Jaws. Jaws boards are a whole other beast," Dollar said. "I needed every inch and every ounce of that board on that wave at Cortes. I don't think any of us truly have the right board for Cortes yet. It just moves so fast, way faster than Jaws."

Two weeks later, Dollar's ride entered the *Guinness Book of World Records* as the largest paddle wave ever caught and ridden.

Photo by Lucia Griggi/Lensbaby

Gerry Lopez Tribute Board

Bend, Oregon, is an odd place for a Hawaiian surfing legend to end up, but Gerry Lopez's relocation from the lush, swell-drenched tropic of the North Shore of Oahu to the high desert of central Oregon can be explained in one word: powder. The greatest Pipeline master of all time is now a dedicated snowboard junkie, and Bend puts him within range of the good stuff.

But surfing was Lopez's first love, and this 7-foot, 2-inch by 19-inch Lightning Bolt—shaped by Gerry and featuring art by Phil Roberts—honors that love. Lopez shaped the board thinking it was to be another Pipeline Masters trophy board (such as those featured earlier in this book). Instead, artist Roberts finished it with an image of Lopez soul-arching off the bottom at the Pipeline. It was presented to him as a surprise "thank you" gift from Billabong. Lopez is seen here in front of the bottom art of the board, at his home in Bend.

Boardless in Seattle

Matt Warshaw poses on the steps of his home in the Queen Anne section of Seattle—looking wistfully west toward the distant Pacific Ocean, clutching his 6-foot, 6-inch Rusty Slayer. "No idea what the dimensions are," Warshaw said. "I liked it because it was a step-up board that I could actually ride in pretty much anything from 1 to 8 feet. Not a great high-performance board, but solid, dependable, good in the barrel. I miss it, because I gave that board away two weeks ago. In fact, I gave my whole quiver away. . . . I am now officially, for the first time since 1969, boardless."

Former editor of *Surfer* magazine, author of *The Encyclopedia of Surfing*, *The History of Surfing*, and just generally the leading authority on surf history, Warshaw likes to have the last word. So the last words in this book will be about him. Matt spent many years living in San Francisco, where getting pounded and barreled at Ocean Beach was part of his daily regimen. He now lives in a nice Seattle neighborhood that looks and feels like San Francisco but is more spread out and spacious. Westport is the place he goes to get pounded and barreled, but it's a mission to get there, and water time has gone down considerably. Matt keeps busy putting his *Encyclopedia of Surfing* online and raising his son, Teddy, with his wife, Jody.

Index